THE
CREATIVE
CORPORATION

THE CREATIVE CORPORATION

Karl Albrecht
with
Steven Albrecht

DOW JONES-IRWIN
Homewood, Illinois   60430

9 4 5 4 9

ISBN 0-87094-929-2

Library of Congress Catalog Card No. 86–51668

Printed in the United States of America

1 2 3 4 5 6 7 8 9 0 K 4 3 2 1 0 9 8 7

The human mind is the last great unexplored frontier—the last unexploited resource—in business. And the potential gains we might realize from understanding it and exploiting its potential could outdistance all that we have accomplished so far.

Several hundred years of progress in the Western business world have brought us to the realization that we can organize, plan, and manage human and capital resources fairly efficiently. We have learned how to orchestrate the factors of marketing, production, and delivery for profitability and growth.

What we haven't yet learned is how to take advantage of what goes on between the ears of the average worker.

We have always known, at least semiconsciously, that most working people could contribute immeasurably more to their organizations than they are ever invited to contribute. Largely because of the unexamined assumptions that underlie much of our management practice, very few organizations ever really extend the invitation. And yet the need and the opportunity have never been greater.

Tomorrow's corporation must *adapt*. It must move with the times, respond to a changing environment, and evolve to stay in touch with the factors that can assure its survival and progress. It is becoming more and more true in more and more industries that the ability to adapt is fundamental to survival, to say nothing of success and growth.

We are now at a watershed in management practice. We have arrived at the point of diminishing returns in the impact of "scientific management." The Frederick Taylor analytical approach of the early 20th century and the Harvard Business School philosophy of rational management which it spawned have worked very well indeed. But the time is fast approaching when we shall need a new paradigm for human organizations that do work. We are going to need some new tricks if we are to keep our organizations healthy, successful, and competitive.

Historically, the management thinking process has always been something like this: define the strategy, set the objectives, organize, appoint the leaders, make the plans, hire the people, put them into their jobs, and keep after them to get the work done.

Notwithstanding the humanitarian pronouncements in the annual reports of many corporations, managers in the United States and most of the Western world are trained and conditioned to see workers as interchangeable, replaceable parts. Like so many little identical stick figures on the organization chart, they are recruited, hired, oriented, placed, and supervised. They do largely as they are told.

More and more the job of the manager will be to manage brains. As the venerable Peter Drucker has pointed out, we have been a knowledge-oriented business society for a number of years. Well over half of the work force is composed of people who produce, process, or transform information in their jobs. Their minds are their tools for working.

Yet management theory and management practice have not evolved to meet this new reality. "Scientific management" has not yet embraced the notion of the worker as entrepreneur, inventor, and thinker. It is a sad commentary on the state of leadership in an organization when a working person says, "They don't pay me to think. I just do my job."

One of the telltale signs of the obsolescence of part of our management philosophy is the widespread confusion and exasperation in organizations about the idea of *performance*. Performance measurement and performance appraisal are becoming more and more difficult as jobs become more knowledge-oriented and less tool-and-task oriented. What we should be concerning ourselves with is *contribution*, not performance.

The notion of contribution as a measure of a person's effectiveness in the job is, in a sense, radical in its conceptualization of working and managing. Many managers have never really thought in terms of the worker as making a contribution—only as doing a job. This, I suspect, is one of the aspects of organizational effectiveness in which the Japanese have the edge on us.

While American management philosophy tends to be tool-and-technique oriented, Japanese management tends to be much more culture focused. Whereas the internal culture is often a resisting influence on American management action, it is often a reinforcing influence in high-context cultures like that of Japan.

All the important signs and many of the important commentators in the business world seem to be pointing to the need to manage in congruence with organization culture, rather than in opposition to it. For the rest of this century, the management of organizational success is going to be all about culture—understanding it, respecting it, shaping it, and reinforcing it along the lines of success in the environment.

We are going to need organizations that are culturally equipped to adapt. They must have internal processes that are creative, generative, and productive rather than controlled, confining, and normative. In short, we must unshackle the human brain and exploit its productive potential.

This will require a somewhat different philosophy of management and a somewhat different view of the organization. Rather than sketch the organization as an abstract system of functional boxes and lines, managers will need to learn to think of it as a live, moving, changing collection of simultaneous productive activities. We still need structure and order, but it must be the kind that enables rather than confines.

The "creative corporation" is, at this point, more a fantasy than a reality. The idea of an organization with a highly adaptive culture that invites and encourages people to use their brains and contribute their inventions is an exciting possibility. It may turn out to be a necessity before long.

In this book I have tried to sketch the profile of the creative corporation, starting with the assumption that it is a good thing to have one. Make your own judgments about how practical and feasible it is to make corporations creative, as we explore questions like: What does a creative corporation look like? How does it act in its environment? What goes on inside it? How did it get to be that way? What does it take to keep it that way? And how is it possible to transform a fossilized, mentally arthritic corporation into a creative one?

I am just idealistic enough to believe that it can and should be done. I am excited about the possibility of making organizational life stimulating and productive for people, and at the same time making the future more secure for the corporation.

Karl Albrecht

CONTENTS

PART ONE

The Problem and the Opportunity

CHAPTER ONE

Creativity: A New Corporate Weapon?

"The ultimate good is better reached by the free trade of ideas. The best test of truth is the power of thought to get itself accepted in the competition of the marketplace."

OLIVER WENDELL HOLMES

Many of today's businesses are making a frightening discovery; they can no longer expect to cruise into the future by continuing to do the things they have done in the past. These are times of rapid change. The price tag for survival in this very turbulent business environment is higher than ever before. Markets change. Technology changes. Social values and tastes change. Industries and subindustries are born and die in less than one human generation. What worked so well yesterday may not even be possible today.

Alvin Toffler's message in his book *Future Shock* is just as relevant today as when he wrote it in 1970.[1] Change tends to produce anxiety. There is a prevalent uneasiness in business-land these days, the creepy feeling that things won't hold still, and that maybe there is no permanently successful approach to the running of a business.

THE ILLUSION OF LONG-RANGE PLANNING

If you've spent much time in or around management, you may recall that "long-range planning" was a much talked-about subject not too many years ago. In the late 1960s and early 1970s especially, it was fashionable for businesspeople to talk about long-range planning with a certain air of assurance. Supposedly, all big companies had to have long-range plans. Infant sciences like long-range forecasting and technological forecasting were coming into popularity. Delphi studies and the prediction of alternative futures were in vogue. Every responsible corporate executive team was supposed to be thinking for the long range.

What was "long range"? Ten years—even if a little amateurish—was considered the minimum time period. Twenty years was more respectable. And for the really big firms such as General Motors, U.S. Steel, and IBM, people tossed around "planning horizons" of 30, 40, and even 50 years.

The ebullient growth mentality of the day even spawned a new management specialist: the planner. All organizations were supposed to have planners, planning departments, and plans. These planners were supposed to forecast the nature of the business environment 20 years out and more, identify alternative business scenarios, and provide guidelines to managers about how to navigate into the future.

Cock your ear for a moment and listen to the current talk. In most cases the chatter about long-range planning has almost completely died out. The lingo of management today centers around terms like "strategy," "positioning," "repositioning," "next move," and "planned change."

Actually, long-range planning never did make much sense. We just thought it did. It's just that today's rapid-change business environment points up the grotesque futility of trying to predict with any confidence a state of affairs so far in the future.

Technological changes make products obsolete, customers demand immediate satisfaction to meet their needs, and everything from production to sales and delivery is moving at a breakneck pace. There is no longer any such animal as a "long lead time."

Surprise Is a Fact of Life

Consider that fundamental influences such as the oil shock of 1973 were virtually unforeseen by forecasters. The rise of the international oil cartel, and later its decline, were not signaled by the regression lines and extrapolations of the management scientists of the day.

On the technology front, the personal computer burst on the scene in the space of a few short years, spawned by unprecedented breakthroughs in microcircuit manufacturing methods. The microchip has had a phenomenal influence on our consumer society as well as on the business scene. Yet its coming, too, was virtually unforeseen by the technological forecasters.

The simple fact is that many of the most exciting changes in our environment have come unexpectedly. Not only the relatively sudden advances but also the longer-wave trends have often caught us largely unprepared. Businesses as well as people have encountered the same surprises and the same changes in their environments. Businesses are having to face a world that is becoming stranger by the day. And it is an unpredictable world in many respects.

Change Hurts

One of the most interesting, albeit painful, happenings is when the entire structure of an industry starts changing. The old roles and rules no longer fully apply. Old strategies and tactics start to misfire.

Hospitals, doctors, lawyers, and bankers, for example, are finding their fields more crowded and competitive than ever. Other service industries such as restaurants, hotels, insurance companies, and airlines are finding that what used to be a seller's market is now a buyer's market.

What portrays this phenomenon better than the household television? For the first time in our history, doctors, lawyers, and hospitals must *advertise* their services right along with dish soap, baby food, and low-calorie beer. It's no longer the "law practice" of Dewey, Soakum & Howe; now it's the "Midtown Legal Clinic, specializing in accidental injury, malpractice, and product liability."

It's no longer the "professional practice" of Doctor Gesundtenflutz; now it's the "Midtown Surgery Center—no appointment needed." The new physician no longer emerges from his or her residency with the birthright of a six-figure income. With an oversupply of physicians for the first time in many years, it's necessary for the new "Doc" to think about "marketing."

Ten years ago few hospitals had an executive position called Director of Marketing. Now it seems no hospital can survive without one. Bed space is abundant and the flow of patients to occupy those beds is low. Hospitals are no longer crowding patients into rooms and scheduling surgeries weeks in advance. With a large number of hospitals in each major city, patients can pick and choose where they want to stay. This means that hospitals must make a concerted effort to compete for business with attractive, safe, and service-oriented operations.

The level of care and concern from the administrative, nursing, and technical support staff, and even the food are now of major importance to prospective patients. People will no longer stand for cold and uncaring treatment, shoddy procedures, or a hospital facility that is not spotlessly clean and highly receptive to their needs. Because of steep competition throughout the hospital industry, medical administrators are being forced to modify the entire thrust and structure of their organizations.

Lawyers face many of the same problems as their counterparts in the medical profession. As a result of the ruling by the American Bar Association that allows attorneys to advertise, many lawyers must market their services or be left out of the competition in a field that has become increasingly overcrowded.

Bankers have many of the same problems. Today you can find a full-service bank, savings and loan, or credit union on nearly every major street corner. With so many banks offering so much of the same service—basically, a place to store your money— bankers are desperately looking for ways to create a differentiated image in the minds of their customers. The days of the bank that just sat there and waited for customers to walk in are over. Today's banking customer wants a broad range of financial products as well as service with a smile, high interest, security, and a sound investment opportunity. Customer loyalty to banks is virtually nonexistent, and banks that continue to operate passively are losing customers.

The point to all of these examples is that

change, upheaval, and restructuring are going to be with us for good.

They are the new order of things. They have become the new norm for the business environment. It is no longer possible to hold course and speed in most industries today. To say, "We've been in this business for 85 years, and we've done it this way for 85 years, and we aren't changing now" is no longer a valid concept for running a business organization.

Toffler is similarly blunt in his book *The Adaptive Corporation*. He asserts:

Some firms are already beyond rescue: they are organizational dinosaurs. These are non-adaptive corporations, many of which will disappear between now and the not-too-distant turn of the century. . . . The very products, procedures and organizational forms that helped them succeed in the past often prove their undoing. Indeed, the first rule of survival is clear: nothing is more dangerous than yesterday's success.[2]

Virtually all of the experts—the management theorists, futurists, industrial sociologists—are saying the same thing: the organization of the future must be able to *adapt to change* in order to survive. This simple fact may eventually become as basic as the law of gravity.

Organizations Are Not Very Agile

Yet almost everything we know about organizations as social-technical structures tells us that adapting to change is the thing they do most poorly. Organizations, almost by definition, are creatures of routine and repetition. Change is upsetting to them. The track record of most organizations over the years, especially of large ones, shows an uncanny tendency to hold course and speed with an awesome tenacity, in the face of abundant evidence that the present course and speed are becoming increasingly untenable.

Some examples? Railroad companies, for a start. During the early 20th century the railroad companies were some of the wealthiest enterprises in the world. They enjoyed continuing growth as the population expanded, the economy grew, and land transport became more essential to commerce. Along came a new technology: the airplane. First came the turboprop and soon thereafter the jet.

What did the train companies do? They continued to operate trains. Already in the transport business, they would seem to have been the logical candidates to incorporate this new transportation technology into American business. Yet they played virtually no part in the transportation revolution brought on by the airplane.

The "big three" American automobile manufacturers, General Motors, Ford, and Chrysler, all watched in disbelief as the Japanese captured nearly 30 percent of the American car market with small, fuel-efficient cars. They believed that the American love affair with the large luxury car, which they referred to as the "full-sized" car, would go on forever. As the oil crisis of the early 1970s played into the hands of the Japanese, American manufacturers scrambled to adapt to the demand for a new type of automobile. It took them a dangerously long time to change their thinking and their products.

The Chrysler turnaround masterminded by Lee Iacocca was indeed spectacular, especially given the circumstances. But the fact is that it was a defensive, rather than an offensive transformation in the business. It was an adaptation made under duress, not under forward-thinking leadership.

The health-care industry provides another classic example of the inability of organizations to adapt, even in the face of dangerous changes in their environment. For many years hospitals and physicians enjoyed the benefits of a business partnership in which they were able to charge high prices for their services, while the intimidated customer—the "patient"—relied on them completely for the determination of which services were needed.

When the federal government moved to stimulate competition by deploying its massive buying power under the Medicare program of medical treatment for the elderly, the handwriting was on the wall. Competition and pricing strategy would be the new order of the day. Yet at the time of this writing, nearly 10 years after the Medicare change became a reality, many hospitals—maybe even most—have failed to come to grips psychologically with the new world. Hospitals are going out of business at the rate of about one per week as they fall victim to the cost pressures of a transforming industry.

The list of similar examples goes on. No industry is really immune. The point is that change, upheaval, and restructuring are the new order of things, and organizations cannot escape the reality of it.

THE PATHETIC CRY: "BACK TO THE BASICS!"

One of the symptoms of the intellectual and psychological trauma brought about by change in an organization's environment is the hue and cry from certain quarters, "Let's get back to the basics!"

The line of reasoning seems to be that the company has strayed from the pattern of success that worked well for it in the past. Somehow people have lost sight of "the basics," meaning the focus of attention they used to have.

In many cases this call for a return to the basics is really a psychological defense measure that serves to stave off the eventual acceptance of a new reality.

Dr. George Ainsworth-Land, one of the most influential thinkers in the field of General Systems Theory, refers to this painful readjustment as the "back to basics bump." According to Ainsworth-Land, when the operating environment shifts and the current habit patterns start to fail, people begin to try other ways of meeting the demands of the environment. This leads to a phase of experimentation in which some people search for new success formulas.

This was the situation in the late 1960s and 1970s in public education, for example. The "new math" was one of many attempts to find a better "product" that would somehow improve the skills of citizens. Many industries, such as real estate, banking, financial services, and health care, have gone through similar periods of desperate experimentation because of changes in their operating environments.

The back-to-basics rallying cry arises when these new experimental approaches fail to bear fruit as quickly as their advocates had hoped and their detractors demand. There is a compelling need to go back to a known condition. Just as a pilot who is testing a new aircraft design always has a known flight configuration that is safe and reliable to which he can return if anything goes wrong, so the traditions of the industry in crisis offer a safe haven. Going back to the basics means going back to what has always worked in the past. No matter that it won't work any longer. The need to go back is overwhelmingly strong.

In Ainsworth-Land's view, this back-to-basics cry is a normal aspect of the phenomenon of change and growth. Whereas most people in crisis situations think of themselves as circling back to a known condition, he believes they are really being pushed along on a coil-like "helical" path. That is, things are trying to break through to a higher level, not trying to go back to the starting point. Getting to a higher cycle on the helix is, in his view, a positive, growthful breakthrough that must inevitably come. Trying to get back to basics is an unwitting effort to thwart the necessary transformation to a new reality.

The back-to-basics bump is the painful period of conflict in values and direction that people must go through in order to conceive of a new reality at a higher level of success. Because the process is usually an unconscious one, very few people are able to conceptualize it as an experience of adaptation and growth. All they know is that it hurts, and they want to go back to something that doesn't hurt.

ORGANIZATIONS MUST LEARN TO ADAPT

The successful corporation over the long run is the one that can evolve with the environment. The people working in it and the people leading it will have to be highly adaptive, psychologically resilient, and open to an evolving reality.

But if change, upheaval, and restructuring are the new order of things, and organizations historically have not been very good at it, something is going to have to give. An intelligent and perceptive chief executive is no longer enough. A strong leader with a hot idea will still run aground if the organization can't make that idea come true.

It will be necessary for organizations to develop *new structures and cultures* that can adapt. That, of course, is much easier said than done. In fact, many corporate leaders seem to believe that the concept of a truly adaptive, creative corporation is a utopian dream.

The key premise of this book is that those companies that do the best job of *becoming* highly adaptive and creative in their inner workings have the best chance of surviving, thriving, and gaining a business advantage over their competitors. Creativity, at the individual level and the corporate level, may become one of the new weapons in the competitive arsenal of business.

At this point it is fair to ask a very pointed question: Do we have any evidence to support this thesis—success through creativity? Are there companies that have made a full-scale, culture-wide commitment to adaptation and creativity, and have they performed better than the opposition? Are there companies that have consistently demonstrated the ability to bob and weave with the times, to reform and transform themselves in a relatively fluid way?

Success stories do exist, but unfortunately they are the rare exceptions. After you tick off a few notable examples, you have to stretch your imagination to name many others. The 3M Company has distinguished itself over the years by an internal culture that values and rewards new-product ideas, many of which bubble up from the lowest ranks.

Texas Instruments has, to some extent, succeeded in fostering an "intrapreneurial" climate that invites people to contribute their ideas. Certain remote regions of the IBM Corporation have a higher-than-normal tolerance for what IBMers call "wild ducks," as evidenced, for example, by the IBM Fellows program.

There are a few other known examples of relatively creative corporations, and most probably some of which I am unaware. But the point is that the list is notably short. You might be tempted to suggest a few of the newer, high-tech companies as examples of corporate creativity. High-visibility companies like Apple Computer, Inc., Compaq, and Microsoft in the computer industry, Genentech in the bioproducts industry, and Turner Broadcasting in the media industry have all had their day in the limelight.

However, the vast majority of these superstar companies are very new, very malleable, and not yet seasoned through the years of the business cycle. In fact, that very newness may be one of the keys to their success. It seems to be much easier for a brand-new company to outmaneuver the older, established industry giants. Why and how this is so forms the substance of much that follows in this book.

At this point in the history of Western business enterprise, we must concede that the ideal of the truly "creative corporation" is as yet largely unrealized. It is becoming more and more fashionable these days to talk about corporate adaptation, adaptability, and creativity. The concept seems valid on the face of it, and it certainly seems to appeal to a deep-lying impulse in the executive psyche. However, the fact that creative corporations are so rare raises certain suspicions about the magnitude of the challenge.

This book proceeds from the assumption that the case in favor of corporate creativity is already established. What I hope to contribute is a realistic picture of the enormous challenge involved, and some sense of what executives must do to make the creative corporation a competitive reality in any particular industry.

NOTES

[1]Alvin Toffler, *Future Schock* (New York: Random House, 1970), p. 2.

[2]Alvin Toffler, *The Adaptive Corporation* (New York: Bantam Books, 1985), p. 8.

CHAPTER TWO

Corporate Creativity: A Contradiction in Terms?

> *"Let us admit the case of the conservative: if we once*
> *start thinking, no one can guarantee where we shall come out,*
> *except to say that many ends, objects, and institutions are*
> *doomed. Every thinker puts some portion of an apparently*
> *stable world in peril, and no one can wholly predict what will*
> *emerge in its place."*
>
> JOHN E. DEWEY

Some would argue that the idea of a creative corporation is really a contradiction in terms, an *oxymoron*, as linguists call it. Many cynics believe that a corporation, almost by definition, cannot be creative. It is legitimate to ask: Is it really possible for a large organization to operate in open, adaptable, creative ways? Is it feasible?

If we're going to have a book about corporate creativity, we had better start out with a workable definition of it. We need to know what it looks like, so we'll be able to recognize it when we see it.

We have to ask and answer some other basic questions right at the beginning. What, indeed, is creativity—in simple, plain-English terms? What would a highly creative corporation look like? How would one operate? Why aren't there more of them than there are? And what does it actually take to make a corporation "creative"?

DEFINING OUR TERMS

Most people seem to have a number of vague, fuzzy notions about creativity rattling around in their heads. They haven't really thought much about it in most cases, so there is little wonder they have trouble dealing with it consciously. They lack a focused definition of the essential terminology of creativity and innovation.

Let's begin with some working definitions we can use in a business context. Let's start with the idea of creating. To create means to *produce something*. A creative person is one who produces—ideas, solutions, inventions, new concepts, and new ways of doing things. Instead of thinking of creativity as some vague, mysterious character trait, let's define it in behavioral terms:

Creativity = Creative Activity

In the business context I define creativity as the process of producing new, novel, and occasionally useful ideas. It's that simple. Creativity is a behavior pattern—a form of activity. Creative people create ideas. All of their ideas may not be blockbusters or best-sellers, but they make a regular habit of what psychologists call *ideation*.

There seems to be a widely held mistaken impression that creative people are all supposed to be "artists" of some sort. They are supposed to be painters, poets, musicians, sculptors, or interior decorators. Many of these types of people are highly creative and many are not. Conversely, there are many creative people in nonartistic occupations. They produce ideas and solutions in very mundane, conventional problem-solving work settings, like corporations.

For the sake of our exploration, let's define creativity as what the creative person does, namely, come up with ideas.

What then, is *corporate creativity?* Corporate creativity is the process characterized by people in organizations behaving creatively, that is, coming up with ideas.

What is a creative corporation? It is a company that values creative behavior on the part of all of its members, at all levels, and in all pursuits. Creative corporations are places that allow, enable, and encourage people to come up with ideas.

This means that a creative corporation is one in which many or most of the people are behaving creatively and successfully most of the time. In the following chapters I will offer a more concrete definition and prescription for making that creativity a reality.

We need one more definition—the definition of a term that many organizational people toss around and yet few really appreciate in behavioral form. That term is *innovation*.

Innovation is the process of transforming creativity into profit.

Ideas are the raw material for the process of innovation. Innovation, in any area, starts with an idea and proceeds through the stages of making that idea concrete, practical, and profitable. It results in a successful outcome, a solution, or a successful state of affairs.

Another way to think of it is that creativity is mental activity, while innovation is the broader process of making that mental activity bear fruit. Innovation includes the process of creativity and much more. It includes all the stages of progress required to bring about a new reality.

It is possible for a person to be very creative but not especially innovative. In other words, he or she might be able to come up with lots of new ideas but be unable to sell them to others or to convert them into reality. An innovator is creative, but not all creative people are innovators.

CREATIVITY IN THE CORPORATE CONTEXT

In order to understand how to make corporations more creative, we must first understand why most of them are *not* very creative. We must be clear about what the creative process is, both in the human mind and in the organization, and we must isolate the factors that operate to destroy and suppress it. Then we will know what barriers to remove, what toxic conditions to change, and what kind of a climate to establish for the development of a value system that fosters creativity.

To answer the question of why creative behavior is relatively rare in the corporate setting, we need to understand how creativity dies in an organization and how organizational cultures resist its rebirth. I say that creativity usually dies because I believe that behaving creatively is natural to the human being. It is natural, that is, unless the pattern of rewards and sanctions surrounding the individual serve to extinguish that behavior.

Children are by nature highly creative, adaptive, and exploratory. Adults by and large tend to lose this faculty. Unless we theorize that some mysterious human gland atrophies and stops operating after a certain age, we must concede that most "mentally arthritic" adults were once creative children who have somehow been "untrained." Their behavior has been reinforced along certain lines and patterns, as they have interacted with the environments in which they grew up, lived, and worked.

HOW CREATIVITY DIES IN ORGANIZATIONS

Creativity almost always dies a natural death in organizations. By "natural" I mean that its death is a normal part of a progression of events in organizational life. This is not necessarily the inevitable outcome, but it is by far the most common. Three factors usually conspire to kill creativity on the part of individuals, groups, and organizational units:

1. Growth.
2. Success.
3. Performance.

These are three very positive-sounding words, and they have great value in the conceptual system of management. And yet the processes they represent are sooner or later the cause of the rigidity, fossilization, and lack of responsiveness that are so characteristic of mature organizations.

How Growth Kills Creativity

Growth tends to kill creativity simply because the elephant cannot move as quickly as the rabbit. Behavior that is possible, allowable, and encouraged in a small organization is often downright outlawed in a large one. As the organization grows, it must pass through certain inevitable stages, each of which adds additional layers of habit, tradition, rules and regulations, and prohibitions. It's just not as easy to get things done in the bigger organization.

There are several specific changes that typically, although not always, take place as an organization gets large. Here are some of them:

Things Slow Down. It just takes longer to get anything accomplished because more and more people are involved. Various departments have overlapping responsibilities, and they all must contribute their portion. The path from idea to reality has more twists and turns in it. Creativity and innovation require results, not just ideas.

The Passive Veto. As the organization gets larger and more "organized," more and more people have "no-go" power, and fewer and fewer people have real "go" power. In the small, entrepreneurial organization, there is more tolerance of the maverick with energy and ideas. The value system typically revolves around doing whatever works. In the larger organization the value system more often revolves around doing things correctly. The culture tends to impose sanctions on the maverick.

Cross-Cancellation. In the larger organization, two or more departments or groups may be competing with one another in subtle or not-so-subtle ways, trying to gain more influential roles. When people start feeling competitive and defensive, they tend to collaborate less. There is less sharing of ideas, less support for creative new approaches, and more preoccupation with who is right and who is wrong.

Nobody in Charge. As an organization grows, it becomes more and more difficult for the chief executive to give personal and intellectual leadership to the others. He or she becomes more and more separated, psychologically as well as physically, from the day-to-day goings-on. There is less tendency for people to look to the chief executive as a role model who thinks up new ideas, encourages others to try new things, and demonstrates strong intellectual leadership. The direction of the company tends to reflect the processes of committee combat, not the inspiration and energy associated with risk.

Various other symptoms of uncreative bigness include:

- Loss of energy due to political conflict, "turf" battles, and combat between "rising star" hero figures.
- The sheer cost of achieving consensus makes the action people cautious and reluctant to go to war on any but the most critical

issues. Compromise arises from sheer fatigue, not from a meeting of minds.

- The cost of opposing tradition simply overwhelms the advocate of some radical new approach. Without sufficient resources and a coalition of thought-leaders to work with, the person with a new idea may never get his or her motor started.
- Malorganization. It is not uncommon for a completely illogical, nonsensical organizational structure to remain in place for years before some energetic chief executive decides to rethink it.
- Loss of a sense of individual identification with the organization. As bigness sets in, the individual tends to feel more anonymous and less motivated to share his or her most precious thoughts and inventions.

How Success Kills Creativity

In a perverse way the more successful a company is with a particular product, service, or line of business, the higher the risk it runs of neglecting its other possibilities. Success tastes so good that it dulls the appetite for risk.

A large mail-order firm I worked with a year or so ago found one approach so successful it almost became a disaster. The nifty technique was the use of a sweepstakes wrapper around the catalog. In addition to offering a variety of interesting consumer merchandise in its catalog, the company offered a chance to win several hundred thousand dollars through a sweepstakes drawing advertised on the wrapper that went around the catalog.

The sweepstakes offer increased the mail-order response to the catalog so significantly that it quickly became a permanent part of the strategy. After a few years, however, management decided to test the response percentages without the sweepstakes offer.

To their dismay they found that the catalog response was not profitable without the sweep. The unassisted catalog didn't bring in enough orders to cover costs. Without realizing it, the company had drifted out of the mail-order business and into the sweepstakes business. It was trapped. It took quite a bit of rethinking and some good marketing theory to get back to profitability and reduce the dependency on the sweeps.

How Performance Kills Creativity

Management professor Dr. Jay Galbraith says, "The organization that's right for doing something the millionth time is exactly the wrong organization for doing something the first time." In many ways a commitment to performance, perfection, and efficiency is a stand against innovation.

Says Galbraith, "In the innovation process, you need to fail—early and often. You need to try lots of things, abandon lots of things, and keep changing the stew. But failure is exactly the thing the efficient organization is set up to eliminate."

What Galbraith is saying is that all the value systems, habits, skills, traditions—in short, the entire mental set of the performance-oriented organization—revolves around doing things correctly. People who spend their days, weeks, months, and years trying to do things correctly in order to maximize operational performance usually have a great deal of trouble with the confusion and ambiguity associated with innovation.

HOMEOSTASIS—THE ORGANIZATION'S FLYWHEEL

Recall the biological phenomenon of *homeostasis* from your junior high school course in biology. Homeostasis is the tendency of an organism to adopt a certain stable configuration of existence and to keep readjusting to that configuration against outside perturbing influences. Just as the human body has a powerful homeostatic tendency, which keeps blood pressure, temperature, and body chemistry all in line, so an organization has a form of homeostasis.

Organizational homeostasis operates to preserve a once-successful state of affairs. The collective response of all the organizational systems, processes and procedures, methods, habits, and value systems tends to pull everyone right back to the "correct" way of doing things.

Homeostasis is not necessarily a negative tendency. It appears in the form of a preference for efficiency, resource conservation, cost effectiveness, and minimization of error. These are all beneficial forces when it comes to maintaining a state of high effectiveness once achieved.

Unfortunately, this very same preference for success tends to bring with it a tendency to reject anything not directly associated with the success mechanism itself. The influential people in an efficiency-oriented, homeostatic company might welcome small, obviously economical changes in the product, the means of producing it, and the means of selling it. But there may well be a collective "immune reaction" to any proposal that calls for rethinking the product itself or reorienting the company's relationship to the customer.

This is still not necessarily a drawback, but it becomes one when the product is losing its strength in the marketplace. When outside forces conspire to present the company with a different environment than that for which its performance has been optimized, its internal homeostasis becomes a liability.

THE ANATOMY OF GROWTH

Many of the internal problems experienced by fast-growing organizations are really predictable side effects of unmanaged growth. We can trace five major stages of growth, based on the size of the organization and measured in rough terms by the number of employees.

At each stage the organization takes on certain characteristic features. For each of the stages, the organization must successfully negotiate a characteristic crisis to break through to the next level of growth. Similarly, at each stage the culture of the organization tends to become less malleable, more stable, and more homeostatic.[1]

Survivor-Group Stage.   This stage begins with the founding of a company by a small band of entrepreneurs. At this point, the company is very small, consisting of 3 to 10 people at the most, with simple roles and relationships and a share-the-work style of operating. The adaptive crisis at this point is a crisis of resources. The business needs money and paying customers to survive.

Family Stage.   At the second stage the company leaders are beginning to find customers and make some money. They've hired some people to help with the various duties—sales, marketing, production, and clerical—and they've moved out of the president's garage and into a rented facility. They now have anywhere from 10 to 25 employees, and a relatively informal style of leadership and decision making still exists.

The company's adaptive crisis at the family stage is a crisis of control. They've begun bumping into one another, and they must establish some semblance of leadership, divide up the responsibilities, and put someone squarely in charge.

Village Stage. By now the company's products or services are selling quite well. Management is busy hiring new people, expanding facilities, and struggling to get this growing adolescent of a company under some kind of control. The executives are overworked, don't have time to think, and are increasingly burdened by problems of coordination and administration. The organization might have as many as 100 people or so by now.

The adaptive crisis at the village stage is a crisis in structure. The leaders must build a formal organization and set up administrative systems that will serve as a framework for continued growth.

City Stage. The organization has grown to several hundred people, possibly as many as 500. It has taken on a fully formalized structure with departments, like "communities" in a city setting. The company's founders are caught up in administrative matters, personnel matters, marketing problems, planning activities, and all the rest of the challenges that accompany growth to such a size. They have become much more formal in their dealings with the employees, only a few of whom have been there from the start. The leaders are hiring and firing people regularly, and the "one-big-happy-family" feeling is fading. The founders are now far removed from product innovation and are fully occupied with running a company.

The adaptive crisis at the city stage is a crisis of strategy. The executives must decide what business they are going to be in over the next years and figure out how to develop and deploy their resources to meet the future.

Metropolis Stage. Eventually the company may reach the metropolis stage, which means it might level out at anywhere from 500 to several thousand people or even more. The organization is now an established, large, fully fossilized corporation, unlike anything it was in the past years. It now has a diverse and highly regionalized structure.

At this stage the company more or less runs itself, by virtue of its formal structure, delegation of authority, and the momentum of a well-established method for developing, marketing, selling, and delivering its products or services.

As you trace the developing structure and culture of a growing company, you can almost sense the process of solidification that sets in. Structures become more formal, lines of communication become longer and more complex, and levels of authority become more numerous and impersonal. As homeostasis sets in, fluidity and malleability fade out. Creativity, in the form of individuals feeling empowered to produce new ideas and solutions, fades and dies as well.

In his provocative book *De-Managing America*, Richard Cornuelle gives an interesting example of what happens to intelligent people who live within an organizational setting and continue to follow the rules, even when common sense tells them something is wrong. According to Cornuelle:

> I encountered a young woman solemnly attending a giant plastic-molding machine. Every few seconds, the machine would clank and spit out a plastic form that looked like a cover for a large cake plate. The young woman would take the part, spin it skillfully around in her gloved hand and then add it to an enormous pile that surrounded and nearly engulfed her.
>
> She turned off the machine and we talked. She told me matter-of-factly that her job was really very simple. She was to take each new molding off the machine and look at it carefully. If she saw no flaw, she was to pack it in a cardboard carton. If she saw any imperfection—a bubble or a crack or a bulge—the molding was to be tossed in the trash bin.
>
> She was puzzled only because the trash bin the management had supplied was so small and had overflowed so long ago. The machine had not produced a passable cake pan for ever so long. But she was comfortably and confidently doing exactly what she had been told to do.[2]

Just about any chief executive who reads this story will, I wager, feel a chill running down his or her spine. The story is all too familiar in so many organizations. Cornuelle's is the story of just about every working person in the country at some time or other. The point is that no one ever gave this working person permission to think. She continued to work at the same pace, either unaware of the futility of her effort or not sure whether she should speak up.

How many times a day does some similar episode unfold in your company? How many people continue to do things the same dumb way, even if it is wasteful, expensive, or inefficient? How does this kind of noncreative craziness become the norm?

You know, most people are really fairly obedient creatures, especially in an organized setting. They are accustomed to doing what they are told. It only takes a few episodes of rejection in a person's experience to extinguish his or her tendency to ask questions, to suggest alternatives, and to notice things that "aren't right." Once the individual worker becomes housebroken, so to speak, he or she just signs off mentally and follows instructions.

A new person coming to work in a particular group soon learns the rules for appropriate behavior. If the other members of the group are well housebroken, the new person will usually tend unconsciously to imitate them. He or she will become housebroken as well, often without ever realizing it.

ENTROPY AND SYNERGY: IN SEARCH OF THE CORPORATE "FORCE"

The problem of leading an organization into an uncertain future demands not only the ability to guess about the future but also the ability to induce the organization to change its ways to meet that future. The first of these is difficult enough in itself. The second is much more difficult than anyone would normally imagine.

I have often noticed during conversation with people who have never worked in a large organization—students, teachers, homemakers, small businesspeople, and sometimes writers of articles in business magazines—how vaguely formed their impressions are about the realities of running a company. They seem to have the most simplistic notions of how things get decided and how things get done. When I mention that I help corporate executives develop strategy and implement programs to make the strategy operational in their companies, such a person will ask, "Why do they need consultants to help them do that? Don't they all have plans? Don't all the people know what they're supposed to be doing?" I suddenly feel very strange. I wonder to myself, "If it all seems so simple to the uninitiated person, why does it seem so hairy in real life? Why don't corporations run as efficiently as the person on the street thinks they do?"

But if I happen to be talking with a person who works in a large organization, and especially with someone who is a manager, there is a different level of perception altogether. Directing a large organization seems fairly simple to the inexperienced observer, yet those who live and work in organizational environments know that there is an enormous gap between the success fantasy in the mind of the manager and the reality of day-to-day activity.

When I studied physics, I learned about an interesting concept called *entropy*. Physicists describe the entropy of a system, in terms of the energy involved in it, as "the amount of energy in the system that is *unavailable for work*" (italics supplied). The theoretical meaning here is less relevant to our interest than the metaphorical meaning. Entropy simply means that no system is perfectly organized, and there will always be a certain amount of wasted energy.

Many organizations are handicapped in their effectiveness by a very high degree of entropy. An organization doesn't exist as an idealized system on a paper, but rather as a human reality. All the people and the day-to-day work they do add up, for better or worse, to what the organization really is. For many reasons, the total behavior of all the people is never fully aligned with the intentions management has in mind for the overall enterprise. There can only be partial alignment in the best of worlds. This misalignment is entropy.

One must sooner or later come to peace with the fact that a company is really a society of people, and that they have their individual and collective motivations, perceptions, beliefs, biases, group loyalties, animosities, and political interrelationships. Theoretically, they all want to do a good job and contribute to the overall benefit of the enterprise. Practically, they usually get distracted by nonproductive issues and concerns.

The head of marketing is interested in marketing, but he or she is also interested in the marketing department's role in the scheme of things. Engineering, field operations, nursing, claims processing, purchasing—whatever the unit and whatever the organization—all have their survival instincts and their political role in the scheme of the organization. "Turf" is an ever-present reality in every organization. Most middle managers want to run their departments effectively, but they also want to get ahead in the organization. They don't always act in exactly the ways top management would consider the most selfless and institutional.

Interunit politics, struggles for influence, and downright warfare are facts of life in large organizations. Most top managers would like to believe that workers and their supervisors want to make the most innovative, creative, and worthwhile contributions they can. But the reality is that they are often distracted from thinking creatively by the most petty, mundane, and unproductive conflicts. They are also frequently hindered and discouraged by the bureaucratic underbrush of rules, regulations, procedures, policies, managerial habit patterns, and traditions.

All the factors just mentioned act to increase the entropy of an organization and make it less productive than it ideally could be. The same factors that stifle and kill creativity also increase the entropy.

What is the opposite of entropy? *Synergy.* Synergy is an overworked word in some circles, but its meaning is perfectly suited to thinking about corporate creativity. The basic definition of synergy is "joint action by two or more forces working in such a way as to increase the effectiveness of each one."

Synergy is the antidote to entropy. It is the opposite process. Synergy means cooperation, collaboration, and the effective interplay of resources. It means that people do not cancel out one another's efforts and contributions; instead, they mutually reinforce one another. Synergy is the result of a shared vision of success. It is shared goals, shared stake in the outcome, and shared responsibility for finding solutions. Synergy is alignment.

When there is low entropy and high synergy in an organization, you can almost feel the energy in the atmosphere. People share a sense of purpose and meaning about what they do. They feel personally connected to the organization as a society, almost as an extended family. They sense that their contributions are appreciated by those in leadership positions, and they feel that what they do counts for something.

This synergy is a feeling as well as a state of affairs. It is almost analogous to the famous "Force" used by the hero Luke Skywalker in the movie *Star Wars.* It is something that is invisible, yet almost tangible. It is largely unconscious, yet it affects the collective consciousness of the people who work in an organization. It can even make a person's job fun.

On balance, entropy is much more common than synergy. For all the reasons enumerated previously, it is easier for an organization to drift into a routinized, fossilized mode of operation than for it to keep the spark of creative activity alive. It is not impossible, but it is quite challenging, to build and maintain the sense of creativity and contribution that leads to synergy in large organizations.

MISCONCEPTIONS ABOUT CREATIVITY

Creativity as Style and Appearance.   Most adults believe, as a matter of simple unexamined faith, that there are a certain few "creative people" in society and that these people are mysteriously gifted with some special genetic trait. Conversely, they automatically assume that they themselves are basically uncreative. In this way they victimize themselves completely because they immediately declare themselves out of the action before they even know what the action is.

Many people who don't have much confidence in their own thinking processes tend to be overly impressed by pretentious people who are not really very creative at all, according to my definition. The kind of person who dresses in unusual clothes, flits about, puts on airs, talks in flowery language, and calls himself or herself creative may actually produce or contribute very little to the surrounding world.

Trying to project an image of being creative is for some people a sort of psychological scam. Because there are very few objective measures of creativity, as there are with mathematical skills or tennis-playing skills, these people just fake it by putting on the trappings of peculiarity.

The acid test of creativity is a person's output. The truly creative person produces a flow of contributions. They may be tangible contributions such as designs, new ways of doing things, or new uses for old things. Or they may be intangible contributions such as new concepts, new approaches to familiar problems, or novel ways of expressing ideas. The real measure of a person's creativity is in one simple question: Did he or she produce anything of interest or value?

Creativity as a Special Endowment. By this definition many people have occasional episodes of creativity, but they usually don't feel entitled to call themselves creative. They can't seem to give themselves credit for their ideas. By defining creativity as some magical trait that is perpetually beyond them, they fail to reinforce their own creative impulses and to let them flower.

So let's eliminate those two misconceptions with the following assertions:

- Behaving creatively means producing new, novel, and occasionally useful ideas, not merely behaving in peculiar, "arty" ways.
- Any human being with normal brain function can behave creatively.

Presumably, we want to encourage creative behavior in some legitimate way on the part of every person at every level in the organization. There needs to be a cultural setting that encourages people to think and to innovate.

Yet many executives—perhaps most—don't know the first thing about innovation or creativity, let alone how to encourage it in their own organizations. Their notions about the creative process and about the means for encouraging innovation are very vague. They often operate from mistaken assumptions and narrow viewpoints about creativity.

Creativity as a Privileged Role. Part of the misunderstanding that surrounds innovation and creative behavior is the notion that coming up with new things is a matter for certain designated departments. The engineering department or the research and development department are presumably the only ones with the psychological charter for creativity. Indeed, there is a pronounced tendency to think of creativity and innovation only in terms of the organization's product line.

Creativity as Rebellion. Many executives are ambivalent about the notion of widespread creativity. They're intrigued with the idea of creativity in general, but they're afraid it may somehow destroy the necessary order and efficiency of established systems.

I was facilitating an executive strategy retreat for a large power company when the discussion turned to the topic of culture and climate. A debate developed around the question of whether the company's culture currently valued and encouraged creativity on the part of its employees. The debate shifted to the question of whether it even should do so.

The chief executive said, "Now, wait a minute, here. I don't think we want everybody in the company to be creative. Certain people have very specific jobs to do. There are some basic requirements of safety and productivity. We can't have them doing the job any old way they please."

My question to him was a very simple one: "Dick, if you had your way, would you want to have each person in the company trying to find a better way to do his or her job?"

"Well, sure," he replied. "That goes without saying."

I replied, "Well, that's a simple definition of creativity—finding a better way to do something. That's the innovation process. We can't tell them we don't want them to be 'creative' one day, and then tell them to find better ways to do their jobs the next day. It doesn't add up."

Dick paused to ponder for a moment. "I guess you're right," he said. "Maybe we're giving people mixed messages. Maybe we're telling them it's more important to conform. We may be kidding ourselves about being an innovative culture."

Now this particular company had in the past developed a number of new approaches to power generation and utility service that they could take pride in. But the executive thought process apparently only associated the idea of creativity with innovations in the product line, not with the more mundane aspects of everyday work.

It's interesting to reflect on the unconscious assumptions behind the CEO's snap reaction to the idea of creativity. He somehow imagined that a creative worker would feel compelled to ignore the established ways of doing things just because they were established. That point of view casts creativity as a negative, rebellious, undisciplined personal trait rather than as a constructive attitude. Presumably the creative worker would value the established way of doing things if it turned out to be the best of the known approaches.

It may be that some executives experience an unconscious sense of conflict when they think about having people at the front line take initiatives in any way. There may be an internal flinch reaction at the vague prospect of loss of control. Vague, archetypal images swim past the edge of consciousness—images of rebellion, mutiny, and disorder.

Even the venerable Peter F. Drucker, granddaddy of management consultants, once wisecracked, "The last thing you want in a bank teller is imagination." Drucker's view tends toward the notion that if top management makes the right moves and allocates resources intelligently, innovation is bound to follow.

Creativity as Something "Feminine."   The business world is still largely a man's world. The primary values of a corporate structure are those of the leaders, most of whom are men. About one half of 1 percent of chief executive officers are women. So for all practical purposes, male values are the primary form of influence on organizational behavior.

Many men tend to consider creativity a feminine trait, either consciously or unconsciously. They see women as more creative, more intuitive, more expressive, and more interested in artistic pursuits than men. Traditionally, creative men have been perceived as somewhat feminine in their orientation, regardless of their actual personal traits. The conventional definition of masculinity and masculine behavior does not include much of an emphasis on creativity.

To make creativity popular in the business world, we will need a definition of creativity and a conceptualization of it as a form of behavior that males can accept as masculine. This would have to be something along the lines of creativity as being clever, mentally flexible, and resourceful.

All the misconceptions just mentioned have the effect of preventing executives and managers in many organizations from realizing the potential of releasing creativity at the front line. It is fashionable to say nice things about creativity in annual reports and newsmagazine interviews. For example, a CEO may state: "People are our real asset," "People make the difference," and

"We believe that the best ideas come from the people who do the work." But the reality is that most executives do little if anything deliberate to capitalize on the knowledge and ideas of the working people.

CAN WE FIND A MODEL OF SUCCESS?

I hope that at this point I have not completely demoralized you about the prospects of the creative corporation. The purpose of our discussion has been to point out that a company needs a great deal of leadership, energy, and imagination to respond well to today's turbulent business environment. If we wish to build and maintain corporations that function effectively, competitively, and profitably, we must have a model of success. We will need to describe the characteristics of success so we will know them when we see them. And we will also need to find a way to achieve these characteristics.

We can describe succinctly the key characteristics of a creative corporation as follows. Such a company can:

- Sense or anticipate changes in its operating environment and conceptualize them accurately.
- Evaluate its own success in terms of how well its internal processes fit the demands of the operating environment.
- Transform its internal processes on a relatively continuous basis to become what it needs to be to survive and thrive in the environment.

Behavioral scientists refer to an organization with this facility for adaptive behavior as a *learning system*. This means that it has the collective capability to learn in order to survive and change.

This is an intriguing idea: the notion that an organization can function organically, that it can be a learning entity despite the fact that it is composed of individuals and subunits.

This point of view suggests that there is, in a metaphorical sense, a "corporate mind" or collective intelligence that can guide a company's destiny. The traditional view is that the chief executive officer and a few of the senior executives take care of the organization's "thinking." Everyone else in the organization is supposed to follow the directions given to them by the executive in-group. But in reality, the employees at the front line know a great deal more about what's going on in the organization and even in the environment than executives typically give them credit for. The consciousness of the organization is not limited to a few key leaders. It is an extended consciousness.

There may be quite a few people who share in the perception of what's going on, and they may even influence the direction of the company in varying degrees. A veteran employee, for example, who has been with the company for many years may have earned the right to be heard from time to time on key issues, even though his or her job definition may involve no such role.

Influential middle managers, too, may play a part in forming the collective viewpoint about what is happening in the environment and what options are available for consideration. Union leaders and influential members as well may be surprisingly aware of the key issues facing the company.

Thus attitudes about the company's products or services may be strongly influenced by the people who are most involved with them at the front line.

All these ideas, attitudes, values, and opinions combine to form the organizational mind. A consciousness of the product or service and a feeling about how best to deliver it are shared throughout the whole operation. This total mental process, not just the executive viewpoint, contributes to making the organization either entropic or synergistic, rigid or adaptive, backward or creative.

THE CONSCIOUSNESS OF CREATIVITY

If creativity tends to die a natural death in business organizations, then it will be necessary to resurrect it and continually nurture and develop it. There will never be a time when creativity will be natural and self-sustaining. It will always need intellectual leadership of the highest order to keep it functioning productively and profitably.

The thesis we come to is this:

Creative corporations will require creative leaders who build and maintain creative internal cultures, which invite creative behavior from individuals and groups.

Our task for the remainder of this book is to eliminate certain misconceptions that stand in the way of developing creative cultures, and to learn what executives and managers must do to make them real.

What is this new *consciousness of creativity* that we will require? What does it look like in the organizational setting? It is a *collective consciousness:* a prevailing ethic, a value system, a habit pattern. It is a set of conscious and unconscious norms that say to people, "If you can find a better way to do your job, by all means do so."

It is a style of working and problem solving that values ideas as a form of capital. It invites, encourages, and rewards people to contribute their ideas as well as their labor. It empowers each individual, at least to some extent, to ask: "Why?" "Why do we do it that way?" and "Why not try it this way?"

In short, creativity consciousness is a mentality in the organization that says to the working person:

"You are authorized to think."

Again, this would seem like a simple set of platitudes if it were not for the fact that so few organizations exhibit this creativity consciousness. More common is a consciousness of conformity.

LEADERSHIP AND CREATIVITY

When the astronauts went to the moon, they didn't aim their rocket at where the moon was—they aimed it at where the moon would be on the basis of the time required to get there. This is known as *adaptive navigation,* and it involves a degree of conceptual thinking. The analogous process in corporate life is the process of setting the direction. It, too, involves a high level of conceptual thinking and a degree of psychological agility.

This brave new world of business we are entering will require certain psychological adjustments on the part of business leaders as human beings. It makes no sense to long for the "good old days" as the company's market disappears, or to grieve at the passing of Camelot as the problems of growth set in. Increasingly, executives will have to learn not only to accept the reality of an ever-transforming business environment but to embrace it with all of its implications and opportunities.

We have traditionally defined leadership as the ability to influence people. I believe we will need to move toward an updated concept of leadership, based on the ability to *influence ideas*. Most effective executives of the next few decades will, I believe, be men and women with very strong intellectual, conceptual, and creative skills, as well as the traditionally recognized skills of interpersonal influence, communication, empathy, and charisma. And they will understand the profound significance of the concept of *culture* in making organizations work.

Organizational theorist Dr. Warren Bennis has studied the behavior patterns of creative executives for a number of years. He has tried to isolate the habits and strategies they bring to bear on the human climate in their organizations and the means they use to shape the ideas of others.[3] According to Bennis, "One of the key problems facing American organizations is that they are under-led and over-managed." He believes there is a *commitment gap* as well as a productivity gap: according to his research, over 60 percent of workers do not feel they or their co-workers give their best effort to their jobs.

In a study of over 90 effective leaders with proven track records of organizational success, Bennis isolated four key factors that he believed made the crucial difference. In his view, "Leaders are people who do the right thing; managers are people who do things right. True leaders are those who affect the culture, who are the social architects of their organizations and who create and maintain values."

The four competencies Bennis believes come into play in leadership as he defines it are:

> *Management of attention*—The ability to form a compelling vision of what needs to be done, and to "enroll others in the vision."
>
> *Management of meaning*—The ability to communicate the vision concretely, meaningfully, and with emotional impact.
>
> *Management of trust*—The ability to earn and keep the trust of those who depend on the leader for direction.
>
> *Management of self*—Knowing one's strengths and special endowments, and using them effectively; maintaining a success attitude and doing away with self-doubt.

When the leaders of the organization have developed these competencies, they can provide the kind of personal, meaningful, and even inspirational direction that people seem to crave. And people who have the benefit of this kind of leadership tend to "turn on" to their jobs and roles with a sense of meaning and mission. They want to give more of themselves because they feel they get more in return.

The challenge of the late 20th century will be to build creative organizations and develop creative leaders who can *capitalize on change*, not resist change. To do this, we will need to become much more familiar and comfortable with the concept of culture and the interplay between change, culture, and leadership. We will need to understand better the internal cultural factors that make the corporate structure so resistant to change and innovation. And we will need to learn how to revise cultures and structures to make them more adaptive.

There seems to be a developing trend toward a focus on creativity and creativity training in business organizations. *Business Week* reported extensively on the growth of creativity:

> Such giants as International Business Machines Corp. and American Telephone & Telegraph Co., along with a slew of smaller corporations, are flocking to the movement's gurus. The companies are packing everyone from top-level officers to production engineers off to training sessions that may be one-day seminars in the corporation's cafeteria at $250 a head or 10-day retreats in idyllic settings that can set management back by more than $60,000.[4]

I do not believe that corporate creativity is a contradiction in terms, but I do believe it is a challenging prospect. The organizations that make the investment in time, energy, and resources to achieve and maintain it will have, in my opinion, the best chance of surviving and thriving in the changing business environment.

NOTES

[1]For a more thorough treatment of the problems of growth, see Karl Albrecht, *Organization Development: A Total Systems Approach* (Englewood Cliffs, N.J.: Prentice-Hall, 1982).

[2]Richard Cornuelle, *De-Managing America* (New York: Random House, 1975), p. 43.

[3]Warren Bennis, "Where Have All the Leaders Gone?" *ASTD Journal*, August 1984, pp. 84.

[4]"Are You Creative?" *Business Week*, September 30, 1985, pp. 67.

CHAPTER THREE

The Process of Creativity

"People should think things out fresh and not just accept conventional terms and the conventional way of doing things."

R. BUCKMINSTER FULLER

Let's have a look at what the creative person does with his or her mind during the process of thinking up new ideas. Then we'll see how that process, extended to many people in the organization, can produce a wealth of new ideas and establish an adaptive culture.

There is an interesting parallel between the way the human mind creates and the way the organization creates. Indeed, the organizational process is an extension of the individual mental process and is similar to it, even though we are comparing an abstract entity to an individual person.

In this chapter I shall trace the sequence of events that makes up the total process of innovation so that we can place the creativity process into its overall perspective. We will see that creativity is the beginning of innovation, and that the effective innovator can carry on through the other stages required to make his or her idea into a reality.

THE FIVE PHASES OF INNOVATION AND CREATIVITY

There are five stages or steps by which a creative person takes an idea from an electrical impulse in his or her brain to a proven reality. Such a person may not always be highly conscious of the process, but it is usually in the background of the thinking process. To illustrate this concept, we will use a diagrammatic model to identify each step of the innovative process at the individual level. Later on, we will see how the process of organizational innovation mirrors the individual process.

As you study this five-phase process, relate it to your own creative experiences. Recall some of the creative contributions you have made in terms of the five phases of the process. Ask yourself how conscious you are of each of the phases in your own thinking patterns. How well do you do each of them?

The five steps in the process of innovation are:

1. Absorption.
2. Inspiration.
3. Testing.
4. Refinement.
5. Selling.

We can represent the process as a cycle which progresses from step 1 through step 5, as shown by the diagram in Figure 3–1.

FIGURE 3–1: The Process of Creativity and Innovation

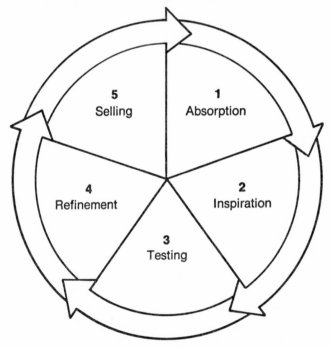

---

1. Absorption—Tuning in to Your Outside Environment. Creative people spend a great deal of their time and energy paying attention to their surroundings. They are enormously curious about many different things, and are continually inquiring into new and unfamiliar subjects. They constantly educate themselves in a variety of ways, such as reading books and articles, talking with interesting people, and going to interesting places. Because they take in so much information, they tend to be well versed in current affairs and they can discuss a wide range of subjects.

The stereotypical image of the absentminded creative genius is largely a myth. Some great thinkers were capable of enormous concentration and could tune out their environments for certain periods, but very few of them cut themselves off from their surroundings as a matter of habit. Virtually all of them were intensely involved with their environments, almost feeding on their experiences as a source of stimulation for their minds.

Even Conan Doyle's fictional genius Sherlock Holmes studied a wide variety of subjects, scanned the papers meticulously, and educated himself on an amazing number of pursuits. His main quirk was that he channeled all of his interests into the study of crime. He was not the Renaissance man, who was educated for the joy of knowledge; he was the quintessential well-informed detective.

Why is taking in the environment so essential to the creative process? Because the creative mind needs raw material to work with. Problems exist all around you, and the elements of the solutions are there, too. If you supply your mind with plenty of raw material—ideas and information—it will process that material automatically and transform it into new ideas and new solutions.

It is interesting to note that people who read very little tend not to be particularly creative. Their lives and thoughts tend toward the mundane. Motivational speaker Charles "Tremendous" Jones contends, "One year from now you'll be the same person you are right now, except for the books you read and the people you meet who influence your ideas."

Creative people are more interesting because they are more interested.

Creative thinkers *absorb* information around them by being open to many possibilities and ways of thought. They get more out of their brains because they put more into them. They routinely take in new ideas, use their imagination, make new connections, and arouse their curiosity—one of the raw materials of creativity itself. The ideas they take in are constantly colliding and interacting in their thinker brains. These collisions lead to the second stage.

2. Inspiration—a Semipassive Brain Event.   Inspiration is difficult to define and difficult to observe, because it happens so quickly and it arises from beyond the realm of momentary consciousness. Once you have supplied your brain with the raw materials for the creative process in the Absorption stage, it begins working on the elements in ways that are largely invisible. Fragments of ideas, bits of information, odd facts, feelings, impressions, and hunches, all float around in the back of your mind, usually while you are thinking about something else entirely.

These bits and pieces may happen to collide in some quasi-random way and cluster together into a concept that offers promise for solving a problem. When that happens, some unknown circuit in your brain rings a bell and forces the matter into your conscious awareness. The flash of energy and the joyous, excited feeling you get are your body's *somatic reaction* to the mental event. When Inspiration happens, you feel almost compelled to dwell on the idea. It has a certain innate novelty for you, a beauty that makes it seem exquisitely valuable at that instant.

People who value creative thinking and develop it in themselves soon come to the point where the Inspiration process is no longer a semipassive event. They no longer depend on the sudden flash that comes at rather rare intervals. Coming up with new ideas, new insights, new realizations, and new options becomes an almost voluntary process for them. They have accumulated such a wealth of understanding that they can react quickly to a new problem and generate a number of possible options for solving it. Those who have developed their skills to that level no longer see creativity as a mysterious and passive process beyond their control. They begin to see it as a rather ordinary skill they can use on a day-to-day basis.

3. Testing.   When you have an idea or a new way of doing something, you must develop and test the idea for its value. People who are effective innovators are willing to put their new ideas to the test, without unnecessary ego involvement. They know that they will have plenty of other new ideas, and their lives don't revolve around the success of the most recent idea they have had.

Testing is a necessary and dispassionate process. If the idea works, fine; if not, the creative thinker asks, "What might make it work better?" This person can accept the successes or the failures of the idea and continue on in either case.

This determination is the biggest difference between the "flake" and the really creative thinker. Flaky thinkers only *talk* about ideas; creative thinkers test their ideas and put them into practice. Creative thinkers learn from the testing stage and do not concern themselves with ego involvement. As Louis Pasteur said, "Others tell you to prove you are right. I say try to prove you are wrong."

Notwithstanding Pasteur's good advice, a certain amount of proving does go on during the Testing period. You must eventually prove the worth of the idea to yourself and to your peers if it is to succeed. There is also a time to stick to your guns as you work with the idea in the face of criticism and discouragement from the idea killers, some of whom may be your closest associates. The key is to be open-minded enough to discern truth and determined enough to persist in trying to make your idea work.

4. Refinement—Removing the Rough Edges. If the idea survives reasonable tests of its feasibility, it still might have some major drawbacks. It might need a good deal of modification and refinement to get it into salable form.

Mentally passive people often suffer under the misconception that innovators somehow come up with an entire idea in its final form in one creative flash. They have no idea that, for most innovators, the real hard work begins when they have the first inkling of the idea. Important ideas seldom materialize as finished products. Most of them need a great deal of evolution, modification, and refinement before they become blockbusters.

When Thomas Edison made his famous statement, "Genius is 1 percent inspiration and 99 percent perspiration," he meant exactly that. Edison was, above all, a *worker*. He knew that having an idea to begin with was fun, but the real key to his success was the effort and determination he was willing to invest to make it work.

The fact is that most good ideas start out as half-baked schemes. Even their inventors know they are half-baked. Creative people understand that they must refine, improve, and enhance their ideas on a continuous basis. Noncreative people see the "failure" of an idea as a reason to quit. Creative thinkers see it as a reason to change tracks and refine the idea into a new or more recognizable form.

5. Selling—Getting Somebody Else to Go for the Finished Product. Marketing consultant Morris Pickus claimed, "Nothing happens in the business world until somebody sells somebody something." The Selling stage takes the idea out to the cold hard world and explains it to the average, convergent, inflexible thinking person. The question you should ask yourself about your idea is, "Can the average guy on the street see the benefits?" If the answer is yes, then you have a salable idea. If that average guy forks over the dough to buy it, you have done a good job of selling it.

PUTTING IT ALL TOGETHER

Many creative people don't have the ability, energy, temperament, or resources to go through all five phases of the process described above. The creative person who can pass through all five steps successfully is rare indeed. Some people can create but not sell, and others can sell but not create.

Many inventors and technical people fall into the first category. Computer experts and rocket scientists can create hundreds of worthwhile products and ideas, but they often have difficulty explaining the feasibility and value of these ideas to other people who may not be knowledgeable in their field. Read through a typical computer software manual as a case in point.

Conversely, many excellent sales and marketing people know little of the technical side of their products but can sell them enthusiastically anyway. The trick to success as an innovator is either to learn to function in all five phases of the creative process or to ally yourself with other people who can handle the phases you don't like.

TWO CASE STUDIES IN CREATIVITY AND INNOVATION

Chester Carlson

One of the rare people who mastered all five stages was a man named Chester Carlson. Carlson's contribution was so significant that, even though he died some years ago, what he did affects the day-to-day activities of just about every white-collar worker in the country.

Carlson invented the xerox process. Working alone in his kitchen, he developed the initial workings for a copying machine as early as 1939. From then until 1944 he tried in vain to find financial support for his idea. All he had at the beginning was a gadget that could transfer an image from a piece of paper onto a piece of plate glass. He believed it could eventually become a way of making copies on paper, but he wasn't sure about the rest of the process.

Carlson took his idea to many potential sponsors and got turned down time and again. Keep in mind as you read this that you are familiar with the xerography process, which is a commonplace part of your working experience. It has undergone many years of development and refinement and its value is now obvious. But in 1939 carbon paper was the accepted means for making copies. It was simple, cheap, and readily available. To most of the people who reviewed Carlson's idea, the copying problem had already been solved. Why go to all that trouble, with plate glass and all, when there was a perfectly workable method at hand?

After more than 20 companies had rejected his invention, Carlson finally found a sponsor in Battelle Memorial Institute, a research foundation in the Midwest. Battelle invested funds and set up a manufacturing arrangement with a small company called Haloid, a manufacturer of photographic products. After an investment of $12.5 million and 10 years of development, the company marketed the first Xerox machine, the 914 copier, in 1959. It was a fabulous success. Haloid later changed its name to Xerox Corporation and became one of the most profitable giants of American business.

Carlson had stuck to his guns over a period of 20 years and had masterminded the entire system from idea to finished product. He died a very wealthy man—one whose dream had become a reality within his lifetime. With an estimated 500 billion copies made each year, the copier business is booming, thanks to Chester Carlson. The main point to the Carlson story is that he made it through all five phases. Not many people can make it "all the way around the circle." Some people have skills in one area but not in another. To make it through all the phases, you need a wide range of skills and a strong sense of perseverance.

Apple Computer, Inc.

In an organization creative people need to team up with others to capitalize on their individual strengths. To better understand this point, look at some examples of companies and people that have used or have failed to use the team creativity concept to get through each of the five phases.

What started out with two young men tinkering with electronic gadgets in a garage turned into a billion-dollar company known as Apple Computer, Inc. Steve Wozniak was the primary research and development person. Because of his electronic engineering knowledge he was mainly responsible for the design of the first bona fide Apple computer and the necessary software. Wozniak went through the absorption, inspiration, and testing phases. Steven Jobs had the ability to take the idea from the testing phase into the refinement and selling stages. Neither man could have done as well without the other.

The entrance of A. C. "Mike" Markkula added another ingredient to the Apple innovative process. Wozniak provided the development of the ideas, Jobs the move up from the garage to the factory, and Markkula the move to the boardroom and Wall Street with his business acumen. Each man added something to the strengths of the others to complete the challenging task of bringing such a revolutionary product as a personal computer to an unfamiliar marketplace.

The early stages of the Apple story provide a classic case study in low entropy and high synergy. The later years saw somewhat more entropy and less synergy as the company made the difficult transition from the survivor-group stage through the stages of family, village, city, and even metropolis. Ten years after the founding of Apple, Wozniak had departed because the large-company corporate environment did not suit his temperament. In 1986 Jobs was forced out of his position as chairman of the board and he, too, left for other pursuits. Apple had left the realm of the small informal entrepreneurial companies and had become a billion-dollar corporation.

One reason why so many Silicon Valley companies burned out and went belly-up was their emphasis on "kamikaze" marketing and advertising approaches rather than on sustained innovation and professional management. During the heyday of the venture capitalists' love affair with computer companies, these firms started small and grew at an extremely rapid rate. Some software and hardware designers who knew nothing of the business strategies needed to survive in the high-tech environment spent millions of dollars of other people's money on wasteful advertising campaigns, Porsche cars for themselves, and paneled offices.

Instead of forming synergistic teams with talented marketing, sales, and support people, many of the company presidents, CEOs, and owners tried to do all of the work themselves. The use of this approach for whatever reasons—greed, ignorance, or the inability to see beyond the present—contributed to the hard downfall of many computer-based firms. You need more than one person in the organization to run the whole show.

More and more people in the Silicon Valley have learned and are learning that it is not just products that make you successful, it's the people and the organization, too. Everyone in the entire organization must contribute his or her creativity to the company.

HOW THE CORPORATE "MIND" CREATES

The process of creativity and innovation in an organization is an exact mirror of the human mind's own creative process. If you look at the start of an idea in an organization and trace how that idea becomes a product or a new way of doing things, you will see that it goes through the exact same five stages of Absorption, Inspiration, Testing, Refinement, and Selling.

For the innovative process to work, each of the five stages needs a role player, someone who can do the necessary things to move the idea through that stage. These stages and roles may not be defined and recognized with precise clarity, but they evolve in any case. One person might play more than one role, and more than one person might be involved in a single role. When all the roles play effectively together, the idea gets a ride all the way from conception to reality.

To better understand the five stages in terms of the roles played by the various influential people, I've given them titles that correspond to the respective roles they play. They are:

1. The Spotter.
2. The Inventor.

3. The Philosopher.
4. The Champion.
5. The Seller.

Let's look at each role individually, and see how it fits into the innovative process in the organization.

The Spotter.   This person is the eyes and ears of the culture. The Spotter's role in the organizational process of innovation is analogous to the Absorption phase of the individual innovative process. The Spotter is the person who recognizes the need for new responses to the environment, new methods, new products, or new ways of accomplishing things. This person can grasp the global logic of the organization's environment and interpret what is happening in terms of what the organization needs to do, stop doing, or do better.

One of the Spotter's best traits is his or her ability to bring back the "news of the outside world" in a timely fashion. This information, which is based on personal experience, contacts with other key people, and impressions gained by investigating the environment, is an invaluable contribution to the collective thinking of the leaders of the organization at all levels.

The Spotter need not be a person formally "annointed" to think in strategic terms. It need not be someone in a marketing or planning department. Anyone with the knowledge and inclination can contribute in this role. A very experienced employee, for example, or one with special expertise or background, can contribute a valuable perspective under the right circumstances.

The Inventor.   This person comes up with many of the creative ideas, options, and solutions for the organization. The Inventor can be one person, a group of people, or an entire department, like the research and development arm of a company. It might be a person who has no role at all in the design of the product or service the organization provides.

The Inventor is always looking for new ideas, technologies, products, concepts, ways of designing something, and new ways to do the simplest task. Often the Inventor develops or creates a new idea or method of doing something and presents the idea to others for review. Anybody can be an inventor, either habitually or just on certain occasions. Anybody who comes up with a new idea can play that role in a certain situation.

The Inventor serves an organizational role which corresponds to the Inspiration stage on the part of the individual.

The Philosopher. He or she provides the intellectual leadership needed to get the right person to sit up and take notice of the idea. This person is a conceptual, contemporary thinker who can see the relevance of the idea to the needs of the organization. Furthermore, he or she has some degree of influence on the ideas of those in positions of authority. They will listen to the Philosopher and have confidence in his or her views.

Often the Spotter and the Inventor don't have enough managerial clout to get the idea beyond the development stage. Unless these people have the right kind of backing from someone with influence, the idea or product may die off at the birthing stage. Also, the Spotter and the Inventor aren't always the best at selling a particular idea. They need someone like the Philosopher to help them.

The Philosopher may or may not be highly placed in terms of formal authority, but he or she must certainly be a person with high "earned" authority; that is, others look to this person as a source of conceptual guidance and leadership because of his or her special knowledge or expertise.

The role of Philosopher is analogous to the stage of Testing in the individual innovation process. The Philosopher tests the idea intellectually first, and then practically if necessary. He or she subjects it to an appraisal of workability, tries to add value to it, and tries to find ways to fit it into the culture.

The Champion. The champion advocates the idea by carrying it into action. This person "champions" or fights for the idea by positioning it as a useful one. The Champion becomes more or less obsessed with the success of the idea and is willing to take personal and career risks by putting his or her name behind it. This person may have access to top management that the Spotter and the Inventor don't have. The Champion may be able to present the benefits of the idea or the concept of a product better than any of the previous participants.

The Champion spends a great deal of time explaining the benefits of the idea to those who need to know about it. It is also very likely that the Champion will try to get access to resources, and permission to proceed with a program to bring the idea to fruition. He or she may become a project manager of sorts, either formally or informally, and organize the efforts of others to carry it through.

The role of the Champion is analogous to the stage of Refinement in the process of individual creativity and innovation. The Champion's role is to make the idea work in the practical realm, and to make the skillful compromises necessary to get it accepted.

The Seller.   This person lobbies for the idea with the people who constitute the operational infrastructure of the organization. Even though the Philosopher has helped to sell the idea to the top leadership of the company, and the Champion has carried it through to a successful implementation, many other people in the organization must embrace it and endorse it for it to be fully accepted.

Somebody has to sell it to the "ant army." These are the administrative people, middle managers, supervisors, coordinators, and all those in similar roles who have lived without the idea so far. It is the role of the Seller to help them buy into it.

Obviously, the Seller plays the equivalent organizational role to the Selling process on the part of the individual innovator.

HOW IT REALLY HAPPENS

If you have worked in large organizations for any length of time, you will probably agree that the innovative process is not nearly so clean and simple as the picture just presented. The foregoing discussion gives a sense of clarity to what's going on, but you won't always be able to see the individual phases and processes distinctly.

Innovation is a very messy process, in general. It is fundamentally a human activity—often a cerebral one—that involves the personalities, emotions, and quirks of many creative people. It does not always work cleanly; it does not always work well; it certainly does not usually work efficiently. After it has been done, people can often look back and see how it might have worked better, faster, cleaner, and more effectively.

Let's try to tie together the people, the phases, the roles, and the outcomes into a realistic picture that gives some sense of the dynamism and human dimension of the innovation process.

First, remind yourself that there may be many kinds of innovation going on, in different phases, by different people, all over the organization at any one time. In addition to the dimension of the product or service, there is also innovation going on in terms of organizational processes, work methods, ways of communicating, ways of making decisions, ways of relating and cooperating, ways of planning, and on and on. In the creative corporation lots of people are finding better ways to do their jobs. Lots of new ideas are popping out of people's minds.

People are sharing their ideas, putting their ideas together with the ideas of others, improving on half-baked ideas, getting certain ideas into specific form so they can propose them for management consideration, getting to work on large or small projects that are necessary to realize the benefits of the new ideas, and even putting the finishing touches on solutions that have advanced through all the stages of innovation.

All of this creative activity, of course, is overlaid on the day-to-day routine work. A person who processes invoices routinely every day may at the same time be experimenting with ways to handle them faster or more efficiently, eliminate unnecessary steps, and reduce the number of errors. Someone who works routinely with customers over the telephone may be trying new ways to increase sales, accelerate payments, and get follow-up business. Someone who ships products routinely every day may be working out ways to apply shipping labels more securely or more quickly, wrap the packages more quickly, or arrange the paperwork more effectively for the customer.

In other words, creative and innovative activity is not necessarily separate and distinct from the day-to-day "efficiency" activity. It isn't as if a working person does something routine all day and then takes a break every now and then to do something creative. And it isn't as if the creative activity has nothing to do with the work. The routine work is the logical starting place for new ideas. The innovative activity is quite properly interwoven with the efficiency activity and serves to improve it in time.

In the creative corporation there is a value system and a set of norms that promote the idea of finding a better way to do things. The culture expects and rewards individual contribution and makes the creative process pay off.

The Culture of Creativity

"Great ideas need landing gear as well as wings."

C. D. JACKSON

If an organization is going to be adaptive and innovative, it needs to have a culture that values, promotes, and rewards creative behavior. This, of course, is much easier said than done.

The notion of culture is finding its way more and more into the scheme of contemporary management thinking, but it still has a long way to go. Very few executives really feel comfortable talking about the organization's culture in the same vein as they discuss its products or services or its relationship to the customer.

Actually, few executives seem to understand the concept of culture in anything more than a superficial, metaphorical way. Many executives and middle managers toss around phrases like "in our culture," "We want to have a culture that . . . ," and "How does that fit with our culture?" But few of them really know how to define culture, how to analyze it, or how to influence it. It is probably fair to say that relatively few executives or top management teams really understand the cultures of their own organizations in any real depth. Many of them are significantly out of touch with the realities of their cultures and are operating under vague, intuitive impressions that may be far from accurate.

As time goes on, it will become increasingly important for executives to understand the concept of culture, to measure and assess their cultures on some kind of regular basis, and to take account of cultural variables in forming the direction of their organizations. What follows is a very brief lesson in "Culture for Executives 101."

WHAT IS CULTURE?

Culture is a social context that affects the way people behave and relate.

Two or more people waiting at a bus stop, standing in an elevator, or eating in a restaurant will feel the influence of the cultural rules that are relevant to those situations. There are ways to behave and ways not to behave. There are implied understandings and assumptions about one another, the situation, and the relationships. Most of these "regulators" of the situation are so well engrained, automatic, and habitual that, while people don't think about them consciously, they have a profound influence on their behavior at all times. People form and influence their own culture on the one hand, and they obey its rules on the other. A culture is a pattern of accepted habits, values, and rules, most of which are so deeply internalized that they are unconscious or semi-conscious at best.

What can we say for sure about an organizational culture? What factors can we identify that pertain to all cultures? And what, if anything, can we do to affect an organization's culture? We can start by describing how human beings establish and evolve a culture, at least in an organizational setting. A culture forms and evolves according to the combined values and priorities of its most influential people. By influential people I mean those who hold positions of power, either formal power or informal power.

At the "micro" level, one person influences another or a number of others to do things his or her way. One forceful person sets the style for a certain thing, and others copy it. It gets to be a standard way of doing things in that neighborhood. Newcomers learn instinctively, by seeing old-timers in action, what the behavioral norms are. They obey, and they soon join the others in expecting newer newcomers to behave properly as well.

Culture thus evolves by imitation, contagion, and enforcement on the part of those who can influence others.

At the "macro" level—for example, a corporation—people who hold positions of formal influence tend to shape the culture by their use of authority. The ways they use power, apply rewards and sanctions, and communicate their personal values tend to affect the habit patterns of those who are directly responsive to them.

The combined effects of the values and priorities of all of these various people who are "centers of influence," on both micro and macro levels, add up at any one moment to the culture. People living inside the culture accumulate, through day-to-day experience, an unconscious understanding of this social context. They carry it with them in the backs of their minds all their waking hours. They take it into account automatically as they go about their daily processes. It shapes them as human actors in the experience of life.

HOW CULTURES VARY

Cultures are seldom homogeneous. They tend to be regional, that is, made up of various segments and subcultures within the main culture. Just as the formal organization is composed of divisions, branches, departments, and units, so the culture of an organization is really a combination of many subcultures. A subculture is a grouping of people who have something in common that sets them apart from others. There is usually a great deal of overlapping in these subcultures, but in certain ways they may be very distinctive and powerful in their influences on people.

Ethnic subcultures usually exist in heterogeneous organizations. Caucasians, blacks, Chicanos, Orientals, and specific nationalities tend to have common bonds of experience and interest. They bring these macrocultural preferences with them into the organization, into their work habits, and into their interpersonal relationships.

There may be many other subcultural divisions as well. Jews, Catholics, New Yorkers, Southerners, people with college degrees, gays, joggers, and the like all have special interests.

There may be male and female subcultures, too. Many organizational sociologists have commented on the "ole boy network" in organizations that tends to work against the advancement of women into positions of authority. Less has been said about the "ole girl network" that tends to reinforce certain traditional behavior patterns in women.

There may be differences in age as well. In some working areas very young people may outnumber the older ones, so the prevailing tastes, styles of dress, and speech patterns may be those of contemporary youth rather than adulthood.

There may be subcultural divisions along the lines of profession or department. In hospitals, nurses usually see themselves as part of a distinct subculture. Physicians do as well. High-technology experts tend to cluster together in terms of their interests and roles. I consulted to one high-tech company in which there was a pecking order of degreed professionals in terms of degree level first, followed by specialty area. Salespeople also may see themselves as a distinct community within the organization.

Some cultures are highly static while others are highly fluid. Most are somewhere in between. In a static culture there is a sense of stability, uniformity, and routine—a sense of things being settled. In a fluid culture things are changing. Rules, roles, relationships, jobs, plans, and organizational structure may all be shifting as the organization goes through a metamorphosis.

Static cultures exhibit homeostatic patterns—a tendency to maintain internal stability, even during times of disruptive changes in the environment. The main features of a static culture are:

- Slow or nonexistent rate of change.
- Uniform, fixed standards of behavior.
- Locally based membership, not transient.
- Resistance to changes in configuration.
- Well-fixed authority and authority figures.
- Simplified values.
- Clearly defined norms.
- Clear application of rewards and sanctions.

Conversely, the characteristics of fluid cultures are:

- Frequent or steady change.
- Flexible, changeable standards of behavior.
- Transient membership; turnover is common.
- Receptivity to change.
- Levels of authority and nature of authority figures subject to frequent change.
- Changing or conflicting values and norms.
- Rewards and sanctions often confused or situational.

It is not necessarily better for a culture to be either static or fluid. Neither is fundamentally more effective or desirable. A culture that is too static may be rigid and unable to adapt. One that is too fluid may be confused, lacking in focus, and ineffective in using its resources. There needs to be some balance point, an equilibrium between static and fluid tendencies.

A static, no-nonsense environment may be quite plausible in the military, a police department, or an efficiency-oriented manufacturing operation. A static culture does not necessarily have to stifle individual initiative or creativity. It just means that there is a stronger need for an efficiency motif. There is a greater imperative to do things "right," for the sake of higher organizational objectives.

On the other hand, a small start-up company may need to be quite fluid for the first phase of its life. The authority figures and roles may not be firmly defined, and the necessity of sharing roles, jobs, and assignments may mean there is little room for a strong sense of uniformity. A static culture in a small computer software company, for example, may be too confining for the needs of the enterprise. A hardened set of rules and sanctions may stifle creativity and establish a negative atmosphere.

WHAT ARE THE DIMENSIONS OF CULTURE?

In discussing organizational culture in management terms, it helps to have some kind of logical framework for describing it. At the risk of running roughshod over the more esoteric sociological theories, we can describe an organization's culture in terms of five distinct factors or *dimensions:* authority, values, norms, rewards, and sanctions.

Authority. Formal and informal clout; the right to say how things will be done; personal privilege; control over resources; entitlement to dispense rewards and apply sanctions.

Values. Beliefs or principles held in high regard. The values of a culture are those things the influential people believe in, stand for, advocate, and work to uphold. Many of these values are unconsciously held. Not all of them are noble. There could be a substantial degree of hypocrisy, that is, of disparity between behavior and espoused values.

Norms. Standards for behavior; expectations placed on the individual about his or her actions in given situations. Norms flow largely from values. For example, a value or value system related to collaboration dictates norms for sharing information, helping one another, and collective problem solving.

Rewards.   The benefits of good behavior; the material and psychological income received by the individual in exchange for his or her role in and contribution to the organization; the formal and informal payoffs provided by the system.

Sanctions.   The punishments for unacceptable behavior; the formal and informal pressures exerted by the organization and its influential members on the person who violates the norms.

WHAT ARE THE DETERMINANTS OF CULTURE?

Each of the five dimensions of culture described above has certain *determinants*, or factors that make it what it is. Let's examine each of the dimensions in terms of its determinants in a typical business organization. Here is a basic catalog of cultural determinants:

Authority:
    Centralization of control.
    Social distance (leaders versus rank and file).
    Obedience expectations.
Values:
    Tradition.
    Morality.
    Business ethics.
    Employee welfare.
    Structure and procedure.
    Collaboration/competition.
    Turf (roles and rights).
    Openness/secrecy.
    Risk-taking.
    Creativity and innovation.
Norms:
    Personal deportment.
    Work patterns.
    Group behavior.

Rewards:

Material compensation.

Recognition.

Advancement.

"Perks" and privileges.

Sanctions:

Formal punishments.

Informal punishments.

Every culture will have its own unique state of affairs in terms of these 22 determinants. That is why, like snowflakes, no two organizations can ever be quite the same. Things may be healthy in some determinants and not so healthy in others. Certain determinants may represent strengths, others weaknesses.

HOW DO WE EVALUATE THE "HEALTH" OF A CULTURE?

There are only two criteria by which to judge the health of an organization's culture. Two basic questions, honestly and objectively answered, tell us everything we need to know.

1. How appropriate is the current culture to the success of the organization in its operating environment?
2. How appropriate is the culture to the well-being of the people of the organization?

Both of these factors go together to make a healthy organization. If the organization is meeting its business objectives at the expense of its people, it cannot thrive for long. If it is catering to the people at the expense of its success in the environment, it will have to pay the piper eventually.

According to the viewpoint expressed by these two key questions, a healthy culture is one in which the authority structures, value systems, norms, reward systems, and sanctions operate to support the success of the organization in its environment and to support the personal well-being of the people in it.

An organization with a troubled culture is almost bound to be operating less effectively than it should. A troubled culture means two things are probably occurring. First, the current climate makes it difficult for the organization to succeed in its environment. Second, this malevolent climate makes it difficult for the people to succeed in the organization.

Lack of success is sometimes a cause of a troubled culture and sometimes a result of a troubled culture. By studying the specifics of the culture in terms of the five dimensions of authority, values, norms, rewards, and sanctions, and their various determinants as just described, we can find out what is wrong.

There are four major symptoms of cultural malfunction that show an organization in trouble. These are the most common indicators of the need for repairs to the organizational psyche.

1. Alienation. A sense of separation on the part of employees; lack of a spirit of identification, group feeling, pride, and involvement. This may involve conflict and distance between workers and managers.

Unionized organizations often face this situation. The steel and auto industries have had this problem for many years. Gaps in confidence or trust between supervisors and front-line people can also create this sense of antagonism. When people don't feel they belong to anything, they no longer contribute; they just work.

2. Conflict. Antagonism and a sense of cross-purposes between divisions, regions, subcultures, work groups, and sections within the organization. When people are feeling competitive and defensive, they tend to work against one another.

In a hospital, for example, you may see doctors aligned against administrators, nurses against doctors, or ancillary service departments against nursing. People may block each other's efforts at innovation, withhold important information, or refuse to participate and cooperate in new ventures because of feelings of animosity brought on by conflict. Entropy increases, synergy goes down, and people lose the focus of the big picture.

3. Despair. A sense of discouragement, futility, helplessness, or ineffectiveness. For any of a number of reasons, people have collectively given up hope. They no longer feel they have a fighting chance to affect their own destinies. The "time-to-abandon ship" mentality prevails throughout the organization.

Workers who are poorly paid and have little job security may just want to "throw in the towel." They don't feel like working very hard or contributing much of their energy to the company. Instead, they may be putting their energies into worry, fear, or job-hunting.

Workers in industries such as aerospace face this prospect frequently. People in such companies as Atari, Inc. and Coleco Industries, Inc. went through this feeling during mass layoffs and threats of bankruptcies as the companies fell out of the personal computer business. Other employees working for Eastern Airlines Inc., TWA, and Chrysler Corporation have experienced these feelings during equally troubled times.

4. Mediocrity. Loss of pride in self, job, product, and company; a prevailing spirit of the times that nothing really counts. A collective "don't-give-a-damn" attitude sets in and becomes contagious. There is no prevailing ethic that supports the idea of performance, accomplishment, personal excellence, or group productivity. In this case, no one cares much about improving upon anything. People just go through the motions, collect their paychecks, and go home. The prevailing viewpoint is "Why bother?"

Large organizations without significant competition or pressure from the environment often tend toward mediocrity. Many educational institutions, public utilities, and government organizations tend to become cultures of mediocrity. Without effective leadership and the threat of external competition, the incentives for personal and group excellence fade away and eventually disappear altogether.

WHY TRY TO CHANGE THE CULTURE?

Inducing changes in the culture of an organization is no small undertaking. After many years of experience as a consultant to large organizations, I have concluded that trying to change a culture even to a modest degree is on a par with trying to turn the *Queen Mary* with rowboats and ropes. It just ignores you.

People, bless their hearts, have their own reasons for behaving as they do. Despite the best intentions and the most grandiose objectives of senior management, they will continue to behave in their habitual ways until something makes it worthwhile for them to behave differently.

The flywheel of habit is very powerful, and it yields very slowly if at all to the coaxing and cajoling of the people in charge. Most of the executives with whom I have worked over the years agree that it is very easy to fall into an idealistic and unrealistic state of optimism about major changes in organizational culture. Experience is a rough teacher in that respect. One must be prepared to approach the prospect of "re-engineering" a culture with a certain degree of humility, realism, and patience.

In any case there are only two legitimate reasons for the leaders of an organization to try to change its culture. They both relate directly to the two criteria for cultural health. The first is that the culture of the organization is in some way inappropriate to its success in its environment. The second is that the culture is inappropriate to the well-being of the people in the organization. If, through a careful evaluation of the 22 determinants of culture enumerated previously, executives decide that certain dimensions need change, then it may be appropriate to undertake a planned organizational intervention.

In the context of creativity and innovation—the focus of this book—it may be worthwhile to try to revise some of the authority parameters, value systems, norms, rewards, and sanctions to make sure the culture invites and reinforces creative and innovative behavior.

After all, the authority and influence of the executive role is usually the strongest single factor in shaping or reshaping the culture.

At Chrysler Corporation, for example, Lee Iacocca took control of the reins and turned the company around during a crisis that threatened to sink it forever. At the worst point, Chrysler was literally hours away from bankruptcy. The Chrysler culture developed a new sense of urgency with regard to its products. Iacocca polarized a large number of people in the company toward the new direction. He helped them accept a new sense of urgency about the need for survival.

Offering the promise of quality products and support through quality service, Iacocca personally became the spokesman for the company in its marketplace. With a series of heroic moves, he and his team lifted the company back on the road to financial health.

Iacocca fostered a sense of "in business and here to stay" with his employees. He managed to change a culture of despair into a culture of pride and commitment. He was able to put the traditional union-management conflict on hold by forming a temporary synergistic relationship with the United Auto Workers, a relationship geared to mutual survival. Putting UAW president Douglas Fraser on the Chrysler board of directors was unprecedented in American business history, but it had the right impact on the situation and the culture.

After the turnaround the new Chrysler had a stronger, healthier culture than ever before. There was more pride and commitment, more sense of value in what the company stood for, and more alignment of people and functions toward the direction of the business. Iacocca became a national hero largely because of his personal impact and strong, values-driven style of leadership.[1]

TURNING THE *QUEEN MARY*

If the senior executives decide on a planned intervention to change their culture, it makes sense for the first step to be an objective, noncritical, and nondefensive appraisal of the current state of the culture. What kind of a culture do we really have? How do the five dimensions of authority, values, norms, rewards, and sanctions look in our organization? What is the configuration of each of the key determinants of the five dimensions? Where are the problems? Where should the priorities be for making things better?

This is good material for an executive retreat. They need to get away from the press of day-to-day business and sit down together to think through what they really want the organization to be. Armed with a fairly objective appraisal, they need to review the health of the culture in terms of its appropriateness to the organization's success in its environment and its appropriateness to the well-being of the people.

They need to choose one or a few specific problem areas for top-priority action. They must be realistic in the undertaking and avoid the temptation to make some grandiose plan that will probably never get past the paper stage. They need to choose a focus for their intervention.

For example, if the executives believe that a sense of alienation on the part of the employees is a prevalent problem, they can focus on that situation. They can begin to search for the causes of those feelings and identify some things they can do to alleviate them. They can make a simple plan for simple, effective changes and get to work on them.

Or it might be that internal conflicts in the organization are draining energy and increasing entropy. They might focus on the nature and causes of the conflicts. They can identify executive actions that can clarify roles and goals and help people find ways to work together.

In order to bring about some significant shift in organizational norms or behavior patterns, it helps to identify the factors that are keeping the situation as it is. A useful diagramming technique called a *force-field analysis* can help with the thinking process. A force-field diagram is usually just a T-chart with *helping forces* listed in the left-hand column and *resisting forces* on the right.

Helping or resisting forces may include organizational policies, procedures, or methods; customer habits; executive behavior; union policies; employee feelings; physical facilities; budget constraints; characteristics of the product or service; and so on. To bring about change in the culture, you can strengthen the helping forces, counteract the resisting forces, or both.

The key is to get down to concrete cases. It does little good to talk about culture as an ethereal concept and to speak in glowing terms of the culture we would like to have. The trick is to identify the specific points of leverage where we can exert influence and cause change by making a new way of doing things more attractive than the old way.

"LOOSE" AND "TIGHT" AT THE SAME TIME?

In their landmark book *In Search of Excellence,* Thomas Peters and Robert Waterman identified a peculiar characteristic of the historically successful companies. Among the eight basic success features they identified, they listed one as *simultaneous loose-tight properties.* By this they meant that the organizational culture demanded compliance, performance, and obedience to key norms and at the same time it permitted an unusual degree of freedom to take risks and innovate. According to Peters and Waterman, "It is in essence the co-existence of firm central direction and maximum individual autonomy."[2]

This strikes me as the prescription for the creative corporation of the future. In such a setting people have the confidence that somebody is firmly in charge. They know that the top leaders have a clear direction and a way to get there. And yet they feel empowered to take initiatives within the context of the overall direction, to find new and better ways to get the work done. This seems to be the ideal condition for synergy.

NOTES

[1] See Lee Iacocca with William Novak, *Iacocca* (New York: Bantam Books, 1984).

[2] Thomas Peters and Robert Waterman, *In Search of Excellence* (New York: Warner Books, 1982), p. 318.

PART TWO

A Crash Course
in Creativity

CHAPTER FIVE

Demystifying Creativity

"I believe that genius is an infinite capacity for taking life by the scruff of the neck."

CHRISTOPHER QUILL

It's time we demystified this unnecessarily exotic concept of creativity. Too many people have the idea that "I'm not a creative person." They suffer from the unexamined assumption that creative thinking is a special gift that only a few unusual people have.

People who don't see themselves as creative often look upon creative people with awe, envy, or amazement. In doing that, they disrespect their own potential. They make an unconscious decision not to use their mental resources and they program their minds for mediocrity.

We need to bring the concept of creativity down out of the ozone and into the realm of the practical. We need a secular approach to defining it, explaining it, teaching it, and promoting it. We need to make creativity "normal" rather than abnormal, usual rather than unusual. Creativity should be an everyday skill.

The fact is that anyone can think and behave creatively, just about anywhere, any time, and in any situation. Everyone has "idea power." It's only a matter of turning it on.

To turn on your idea power, you first have to realize it's there. You have to learn to see creativity in yourself, appreciate it, reward and reinforce yourself for it, and recognize the value it has in your life. As you go through a typical day, pay attention to your responses to problem situations. Notice the times when you respond open-mindedly to new information. Notice when you consciously recognize the various points of view in a situation. Notice when you consciously seek options to solve some problem, rather than respond by habit in terms of only one way of doing things.

Each time you respond creatively and flexibly to a problem, make a conscious note of your actions. Consciously give yourself credit for using your creative mental functions. Call yourself a creative person. The more you do this, the more it will seem normal. Eventually, your mind will accept the idea of your being a creative person, and you will begin to make creativity a part of your habit patterns.

THE CHARACTERISTICS OF CREATIVITY

The way to join the ranks of creative, innovative thinkers is to find out what they do and then imitate them. In other words, by adopting the behaviors of creativity, you become more creative. That's all there is to it. You don't need a magical transformation of your cell structure, and you don't need to be specially "anointed" for creativity. You just start *doing* it.

Think about some of the famous figures in our history and note which ones were masters at thinking creatively. What names come to your mind? People like Albert Einstein, Thomas Edison, and R. Buckminster Fuller may occur to you immediately. How about Leonardo da Vinci? Martin Luther? Shakespeare? Marie Curie? Thomas Jefferson? Thoreau? Frank Lloyd Wright? John Dewey, educator? How about Henry Ford? Gandhi? Florence Nightingale? Mark Twain? Winston Churchill?

What personal characteristics did these famous thinkers have in common? These people and others like them developed the habit of thinking in such new and refreshing ways that they were able to make fundamental contributions to the times in which they lived.

It was their ability to produce and present new and valuable ideas that made them all so outstanding in their respective fields of endeavor. These people had the courage to develop and articulate their ideas, even when their peers scoffed at them. And most of them had very flexible and adaptable outlooks on life with respect to the way they critically examined the culture around them.

Even though the people named above worked in very different sectors of life and in different times, some common characteristics make them similar. The skill pattern of creativity is not at all haphazard. It is not a random mixture of random traits. If you examine the actions of high-powered thinkers, you can spot certain key things they do. Certain key habits of thought serve them well and enable them to make important contributions while their peers stand and watch.

These creative thinking factors are learned, not inherited. You can think in this way too, once you know how to go about it and once you decide you want to.

One might argue that the really famous thinkers of our history have been unusual people, gifted with certain genetic traits. They were mutations perhaps, and not really plausible role models for the rest of us. I prefer to leave that particular argument to the sociologists. I do know, however, that I have learned how to do many of the same things that these famous thinkers have done, and I have seen the results in my own life and career. And I have taught many other people to do the same in creativity seminars.

There are five basic characteristics that make the difference for innovative and creative thinking. We all have these characteristics to some extent, but the great thinkers in our world *really* have them. They have made these attitudes and habits of thought a basic part of their approach to living. I'll explain each one in detail in the chapters that follow. They are:

1. Mental flexibility.
2. Option thinking.
3. Big-picture thinking.
4. Skill in explaining and selling ideas.
5. Intellectual courage.

Now think again about some of the great thinkers in our history. Which of these characteristics do you recognize in people like Winston Churchill, Mark Twain, Albert Einstein, and Thomas Edison? While they were not all skilled in all of the five areas just mentioned, all were well versed in at least several of them.

Think about the people you deal with every day at work. Which of these people do you see as truly innovative, creative thinkers? Do those people seem normal to you or have you always felt that they have some special gift? Can you see their creative skills in terms of the five key mental habits enumerated above?

How do you see yourself on the creativity scale? Do you make use of the key habits of creativity? How do other people see you?

While I've devoted an entire chapter to each of the five factors in the creativity prescription, here is a brief overview of each of them.

Mental Flexibility

Mental flexibility is the basis of all effective problem solving. The term itself denotes a certain sense of adaptability in your thought processes. It is a practiced method of thinking that enables you to be adaptable and flexible in the ways in which you approach a particular problem. From a psychological standpoint it is the ability to keep your mental outlook changeable. Mentally flexible thinkers allow themselves to be influenced by new angles or opinions.

This mental flexibility involves, for example, a characteristic psychologists call a *tolerance for ambiguity*, which enables you to deal comfortably with situations that are complex, unresolved, and not amenable to simple solutions. The ambiguous problem situation requires you to wait until the situation resolves itself before you know what options are available and what outcomes may be feasible.

A closely related factor is the ability to defer judgment in a given situation, which means that you don't always have to decide yes or no right away. There is usually time to consider the various options in all but the most life-threatening problems.

Thomas Edison, Galileo, Copernicus, da Vinci, Marconi, and a score of other famous inventors were mentally flexible thinkers. They could bend and adapt to accept new information or discoveries. They withheld their judgment about a concept until they understood all of the facts and considered all of the options available.

Option Thinking

Great thinkers can generate ideas. They are option thinkers who can see a wide variety of solutions for simple or complex problems. They can generate ideas like popcorn, one right after the other.

There is a simple philosophy behind option thinking. It is the notion that:

The way to have good ideas is just to have plenty of ideas.

If you constantly think in terms of "ways" rather than "the way" of doing things, you make a habit of letting your ideas flow. You keep your mental popcorn machine going all the time. You don't demand that every idea that comes out of your mind be a block-buster invention. You just keep your ideas coming. Some of them are bound to be blockbusters. Many of the rest will be useful. Who cares that not all of them are great?

Thomas Edison once said that he tried over 700 different types of materials to use as a filament for his light bulb before he came up with the most effective one. Before he discovered the right material for the filament, someone asked him if he thought he had failed. He replied succinctly, "Of course not. Now I know 700 things that won't work."

This capacity to generate new and plentiful ideas expands your capacity to solve problems. By generating a wide range of ideas, you also generate a wide range of possible solutions. The more options you have to choose from, the better equipped you are to solve any problem. You can always discard the options or ideas that aren't feasible at a later time.

Big-Picture Thinking: The Helicopter View

Another key characteristic of creative thinkers is their capacity to think conceptually. In order to think conceptually, you must be able to take what I refer to as the *"helicopter view"* of problem solving. Just as a helicopter can hover above ground and see the total picture, you need to be able to step back and look at the whole problem to be solved.

Conceptual thought is also called *global thought*, because global thinkers can see a whole world of creative possibilities. Conceptual thinkers can see "the forest through the trees." They know that for each problem, there is a focused view and an overall view. The ability to see the overall view helps you to broaden your capacity to solve a problem. After the helicopter view allows you to see the entire problem, you can narrow the possible solutions to a select number and begin to concentrate on the finer points of the problem-solving process.

Global thinkers can also see the possible impact of certain solutions to a problem. At the corporate level, the conceptual thinker can see that his or her solution for a complex sales problem might have an impact on the product or service a year down the line. The global thinker in this case knows enough about the scope of the problem to see into the future and to think relationally.

Winston Churchill, Franklin Roosevelt, and John Kennedy were global, conceptual thinkers. They dealt with problems on such a large scale that they were forced to look around and look ahead to see the possible ramifications of their decisions.

Global thinking, helicopter thinking, conceptual thinking—call it whatever you like. The point is that your personal capability to solve problems and the impact you have on the ideas of others is significantly related to your skill at processing the big picture. If people see you as a skilled conceptual thinker, and not one who gets mired in the mundane details, they tend to rely on your views and approaches. They see you as a high-powered thinker and someone who has an important contribution to make.

Explaining and Selling Your Ideas

It is not enough to have great ideas. Unless you can sell your ideas to other people, especially those in positions of influence, you'll never get them off the ground. There are plenty of frustrated, discouraged "idea people" in almost any corporate setting. These are the people who have good ideas but can't explain them, dramatize them, or make them come alive for other people. Effective innovators are the people who can get inside the heads of others and rearrange their understanding.

Think of some of the highly articulate people of our time, such as William F. Buckley, Edwin Newman, and Carl Sagan. Many people consider Ronald Reagan one of the most effective of all American presidents at explaining things to the public in dramatic, compelling ways. These people all have a command of the language that allows them to express themselves in a very impressive manner. They can get their point across by using just the right well-turned phrase or concept. They all seem to the listener to possess a clarity of thought and an ease of expression that helps them convey their ideas in an articulate, fluent, and often powerful manner.

In the creative corporation articulate men and women are also seen as having power. The ability to express yourself with clarity, ease, and skill goes a long way toward helping others see you as someone who counts. Your command of the written and spoken word can be just as important a factor in your influence with others as the content of your knowledge.

Intellectual Courage: Sticking to Your Guns

The last of the five characteristic mental habits of the creative thinker is intellectual courage. This is the ability to advocate an unpopular idea in the face of apathy, rejection, defensiveness, narrow-mindedness, bigotry, and even hostility from others who don't understand it and can't embrace it.

Much of the history of scientific progress revolves around breakthroughs in concept, consciousness, or technology that didn't look like breakthroughs at the time. The majority of people can't picture something they haven't seen before. A new way of doing something, an entirely new way of defining a problem, or a new option no one has seen tried before usually triggers an automatic rejection reaction deep in their unconscious thinking patterns. It is quite common for people who don't think very much to respond with, "If that idea were any good, why hasn't somebody already done it?"

There are more idea killers than there are idea thinker-uppers in any society. In the corporate setting especially, the typical norms around conventional ways of doing things usually condition people to shoot down the new and unfamiliar because they don't feel comfortable with the temporary ambiguity that it creates.

The effective innovator must be able to live, work, walk, talk, and survive among the normal thinkers that populate the corporate landscape. If you are going to succeed through creativity and innovation, you must develop the communication skills to sell ideas to others and the intellectual courage to persist in your course until they eventually do understand what you are trying to create.

THE POWER OF CREATIVITY

If you can incorporate these five key habit patterns into your thinking processes, you can become not only a creative thinker but an effective innovator. Not only will you have more ideas that are new, novel, interesting, exciting, and potentially useful but you will also gain influence over the ideas of others.

Your goal is to have others see you as effective, not just creative. By developing the ability to think up new ideas, sell those ideas to others, and carry them through into useful form, you can become one of the key thought-leaders of your organization.

CHAPTER SIX

Mental Flexibility

*"Compared to what we ought to be, we are only half awake.
We are making use of only a small part of our physical and
mental resources."*

WILLIAM JAMES

Mental flexibility is one of the primary hallmarks of the creative thinker. It is an orientation, an attitude, a habit pattern, and a way of reacting to experience. A mentally flexible person approaches each new situation, problem, or exchange of ideas with an attitude we can characterize as *intellectually innocent*. That is, such a person is relatively free of preconceived interpretations, fixed opinions, negative value judgments, prejudice, or dogmatic positions. He or she is willing to *learn* moment by moment and be open to the ideas of others.

The mentally flexible person is able to defer or suspend value judgments at will, confident that he or she can thereby make more enlightened judgments when the situation calls for them. By being flexible and open to the possibilities in a situation, this person perceives things more accurately than a narrow-minded person and can take a much broader approach to solving any particular problem.

Mental flexibility is something that all effective problem solvers have in common. By definition, flexibility refers to your ability to *adapt* to various situations. Being mentally flexible means that you have the capacity to accept new or different ways of looking at the situation, new interpretations of the status quo, and new ways of going about things.

From a psychological standpoint, mental flexibility is the ability to keep your mental outlook changeable. You need to be willing to modify your opinions as you encounter more information and discover new angles to a problem.

THE ELEMENTS OF MENTAL FLEXIBILITY[1]

We can delve more deeply into this important attitude of mental flexibility and describe it more concretely. The flexible thinker has certain specific characteristics and habits of thought we can analyze and learn. I have identified seven major factors that seem to go together to make a person mentally flexible. They are:

1. A Tolerance for Ambiguity.   The ability to deal comfortably with unresolved, uncertain, and unfamiliar situations.

2. Opinion Flexibility.   The ability to keep your opinions "on probation" most of the time, to suspend your judgment until later, and to appreciate the points of view of others.

3. Semantic Flexibility.   Using semantically flexible language habits, avoiding dogmatic, rigid statements and unnecessary figures of speech as you express your ideas.

4. Positive Orientation.   The ability to maintain a positive frame of mind, look at your life experiences in terms of successful expectations, and keep your emotions on an even keel most of the time.

5. Sense of Humor.   The ability to see the lighter side of life, not to take yourself or others too seriously, and to use humor in a constructive manner.

6. Investigative Orientation.   A respect for evidence; the acquired habit of seeking out new and relevant information.

7. Resistance to Enculturation.   The ability to look at your surroundings and culture with an open mind, and decide for yourself which of the prevailing values and beliefs are valid for you.

Let's look at each of these characteristics in turn.

Tolerance for Ambiguity

An ambiguous situation is one that does not present an easily recognizable solution. There may be too wide a range of options, or the options may not be apparent without further study. People who have trouble with ambiguous situations find it difficult to wait things out. Their overdeveloped need for structure and order in their lives makes them uncomfortable with unresolved situations. They tend to get nervous, apprehensive, or even irritable if they don't have "the answer."

Aggressive people, especially those with the well-known Type A behavior pattern, often become extremely frustrated and impatient when they confront highly ambiguous problem situations. Some people are psychologically disabled by extreme ambiguity in their personal situations.

The reality of life is that to think and work creatively, you must be willing to accept ambiguity as a normal part of the situation. Ambiguity is not necessarily bad. It just means that a specific solution either is not quite apparent or will require more study and effort.

In the organizational setting, ambiguous situations present themselves on a daily basis. Problems arise that you just can't solve without further study or a commitment of resources, information, or time. Long-term situations that don't have easy answers sometimes leave you no choice but to "ride to the sound of the guns."

Creative thinkers don't fear ambiguity; they acknowledge it, accept it, and work with it. They realize it is often a necessary part of the inner workings and problem-solving processes of any business environment.

Opinion Flexibility

"Opinionitis" is one of the most self-limiting and potentially dangerous afflictions of the human species. The French philosopher Voltaire contended that "opinion has caused more trouble on this little planet than plagues or earthquakes." He was correct (in my opinion).

Most people take it as an article of faith that one should have and defend strong opinions. We are brought up in a culture that values being right, even at the risk of being wrong. Among males, for example, it is considered manly to have made up your mind about something and to defend it stoutly in verbal combat with others. Many men, and women as well, are afraid others will consider them weak, wishy-washy, and lacking in guts if they admit to ever changing their minds.

Our culture tends to admire people who are good at debating, which is not a communication process at all but a form of combat. No self-respecting debater would stop in the heat of battle and say, "By Jove! I believe you're right. I hadn't really considered that point before. Thank you for helping me see it more clearly." This would be tantamount to intellectual suicide and would certainly lead to dismissal from the debating team.

There are times when it is important to take a stand and advocate something strongly, and there are times when it is important to listen and learn. On the one hand, if a person never takes a stand on anything, he or she will probably accomplish very little. On the other hand, a person who forms rigid opinions, refuses to ever re-evaluate them, and defends them against all onslaughts of fact and logic blocks his or her own adaptation. There is a valuable middle ground between never believing in anything and never being willing to rethink your point of view. This middle ground is opinion flexibility.

People who are flexible in their opinions can do three things effectively. First, they can defer their judgments until they have access to all the relevant facts and views that can help them form their opinions effectively. They can solidify their opinions consciously and deliberately rather than as a snap reaction to limited evidence.

Second, they can reassess their opinions and their points of view without undue defensiveness or ego involvement. They place a higher value on learning and adapting than they do on making other people "wrong" and themselves "right." They are willing to approach an exchange of views as a contest of ideas rather than a contest of personalities.

And third, they can actually change their minds, confidently, nondefensively, and gracefully. They take no shame in acknowledging that they have been wrong in a given situation, and they can appreciate a better way of looking at things. They can even give credit to others for helping them learn and grow.

Think about your own opinion-making habits. Do you suffer from opinionitis to some extent? How open are you to new viewpoints, new interpretations of a situation, and new courses of action? What does it take for you to change your mind—dynamite? Or new evidence that sheds new light on the situation?

By consciously *managing* your opinions and keeping them "on probation" most of the time, you can maintain a state of psychological readiness that enables you to change your point of view if the evidence warrants it. At the same time you can act on your current beliefs with the confidence that you have thought them through and given yourself the benefit of the best evidence and the most enlightened points of view available to you.

Semantic Flexibility

Creative thinkers are also *semantically flexible* thinkers. If you listen carefully to the conversation of a highly creative, innovative person, you will very likely hear an unusually low incidence of rigid, dogmatic, and absolutist terminology. Instead, you will probably hear a high proportion of semantically flexible terms and sentence structures. A semantically flexible structure is one in which the choice of words telegraphs an openness to acknowledge other facts and evidence, other points of view, and other ways of interpreting the situation.

The *language habits* you've developed over the course of your life have a very strong influence on the way you perceive the world and the way others perceive you. By expressing your perceptions and viewpoints in a semantically flexible way, you invite others to feel comfortable in exchanging views with you. Just as important, you invite your own brain to process your ideas more flexibly and creatively.

People who are semantically rigid in their thinking patterns and rigid in their means of expressing themselves often habitually rely on what linguists call *all-ness language forms*. These include expressions like "*Everybody* needs a computer," "*Nobody* cares about that," "You *always* do such-and-such," and "That will *never* work." Sometimes the all-ness term is fully warranted by the facts, but many times it just pops out as a symptom of an oversimplified, rigid habit of thought on the part of the speaker.

Other semantically rigid patterns include the overuse of *two-valued expressions* that cast a situation in terms of only two opposing options. Two-valued thinking and talking fails to recognize the spectrum of possibilities that is often inherent in a situation.

For example, a person might say, "Well, there are always two sides to every argument." In fact, it seems to make more sense to say that there are many potential sides. When a person asks, "Are you with us or against us?" he or she is truncating the range of options offered to the listener to just two. Both of them might be unattractive, and there may be other interpretations that would make more sense for the listener.

Verbal dogmatism is a very common form of semantic rigidity. When a person says, "That's a stupid way to do it," or "That's wrong," or "Our customers will never buy that," he or she is bludgeoning the listener with an opinion, with no acknowledgment that the listener might be entitled to a different point of view. Dogmatism tends to cause the listener to react somewhat defensively on an unconscious basis, and to see the speaker as aggressive and "pushy," and not receptive to his or her views.

The antidote to verbal dogmatism is called "to-me-ness," and it is a verbal pattern that recognizes the inescapable fact that the speaker can only speak from his or her own personal experience and point of view. When you say "It seems to me that . . ." or "In my opinion, . . ." or "So far as I know, . . ." you are acknowledging that you are giving your own outlook and interpretation of things. You are implicitly telegraphing to the other person that you are willing to acknowledge, if not agree with, his or her point of view.

Value-labeling is another form of semantic rigidity. It is such a common verbal habit in our culture that we tend to be relatively unaware of it. Much of this misuse comes when we label other people in order to categorize their appearance, behavior, or actions in our own minds. Describing a person with words like *hippie*, *dirtbag*, *redneck*, *crook*, *pig*, or *lamebrain* creates an evaluative bias that colors one's further perceptions of the person.

Semantically flexible people try to describe other people in terms that are less value-laden and more objective in order to keep their own feelings as neutral as possible. They don't have to like everybody, but they realize that value-judging people leads to rigid, programmed ways of reacting to them.

Changing the way you speak about yourself is also an important part of semantic flexibility. If you talk down about yourself to other people, then they will begin to see you in that way too. Negative thoughts and expressions about yourself reinforce this opinion in the minds of the people who deal with you. In an organizational situation, this type of negative self-description can be damaging to your influence with others whose support you need.

Conversely, if you clean up your "language act," refer to yourself in more positive terms, and speak highly of your skills and abilities—in a nonthreatening, low-key manner—then other people will begin to see you as more confident and self-assured. Why undermine your effectiveness with negative comments about yourself?

One further point about semantic flexibility. Many studies of group dynamics have shown that most people tend to see the semantically flexible person as more intelligent, a clearer thinker, a more effective problem solver, and a more trustworthy leader than the person who is rigid, dogmatic, and aggressive in his or her language patterns. You can add a measure of effectiveness to your relationships with others by making your language habits the habits of creativity and semantic flexibility.

Positive Orientation

The mentally flexible person is willing and able to approach life from the positive angle. This person's "optimism quotient" is very high on the average. He or she operates on the basic belief that a confident attitude, belief in self, and positive expectations will pay off more than a fearful approach based on negative expectations.

People who have a very negative outlook on life usually feel helpless, ineffective, and powerless. The expectation of failure and disappointment tends to be self-fulfilling because they don't act against their problems with sufficient energy and commitment.

Conversely, people who have a basically positive outlook tend to experience success and satisfaction because they believe that's what will happen. Thoughts are very powerful things. Whatever we focus our thoughts on is what we tend to produce in our lives.

People who have a high positive orientation are not necessarily gushy or preachy about it. They just maintain a matter-of-fact point of view about success. They believe they deserve it, they expect it, and they make it happen because they allow no other possibilities to distract them. Nor are they necessarily naive pushovers in business. They recognize that not everyone is honest or trustworthy, but they start with the anticipation of honesty and fair play. They act as if they expect everyone else to be honest, and that expectation often has a strong influence on the behavior of others.

Think about your own mental and emotional orientation. Are you able to maintain a positive outlook most of the time and program your expectations for success in most situations? Or do you worry, complain, criticize yourself and your assets, and declare failure before you begin? Do you make a habit of focusing your energies on success and not worrying about failure?

Sense of Humor

Laughter is the sunshine of the soul. It uplifts us, puts us in touch with our higher selves, and reminds us of our real potentialities as human beings. It makes us feel better, and in feeling better we find it easier to treat others with consideration and humanity. A good rule for living is:

Don't pass up a chance to have a good laugh.

A well-developed sense of humor is truly a sanity skill in today's world. It keeps you in touch with the lighter side of life. The ability to be amused by the large and small things in daily life helps to minimize stress, keep you mentally agile, and keep you feeling good most of the time.

Most creative thinkers tend to see the world as basically a funny place. Although they acknowledge that there are many problems in the world, they see no value in having their own emotions dragged down by ruminating unproductively on the negative side of life. While many tragic figures in history have contributed creative new ideas, the people with a sense of humor in their lives have been the ones who were more well-rounded and successful as individuals.

People who won't let themselves laugh and enjoy the funny side of life pay a high price for living. We have all seen the hard-driving, workaholic businessperson—the one who takes no vacations, chain-smokes, drinks too much, and works 12 hours a day. How often do you see this person really unwind and laugh at some amusing episode of life and genuinely enjoy it? Probably not very often, because these people have lost one of life's greatest gifts: the sense of humor.

If you think about your psychological reactions, especially when you are under a great deal of pressure, you will probably find that the most reliable indication of being overstressed is that you tend to lose your sense of humor. The world is no longer a funny place when your stress level is high. This one barometer alone can help you keep in touch with your feelings and keep yourself in a positive emotional state most of the time.

This doesn't mean that laughing will solve the world's problems, but it will allow you to look at them with a better feeling of confidence and optimism.

Psychologists recognize a three-way correlation between positive orientation, sense of humor, and the ability to think up new ideas. They seem to be intertwined somehow, as if they spring from the same internal, psychological well in the person. People with a well-developed sense of humor tend to come up with ideas more frequently, more fluently, and more effectively than those for whom life seems to be a terminal illness.

In the creative corporation there must be room for a sense of humor, even in a business environment. This doesn't mean that people stand around and tell jokes all day, but neither should they feel that they have to check their sense of humor at the front door of the building. When humor and a sense of the light touch are part of the psychological landscape in the organization, people feel connected, involved, energized, and empowered to put themselves into what they do.

Investigative Orientation

The *investigative orientation* is the habit of being "scientific" about solving problems. It means seeking information, understanding, and enlightenment as a preparation for effective decisions. The investigative orientation is a respect for evidence. It is a belief in the value of the process of investigation itself as a source for better options and greater comprehension of any given problem situation.

Probably a majority of people, even those with college-level education, tend to rely on hearsay, assumption, and unsupported conjecture in forming their impressions of a situation. For example, many executives will launch internal programs or campaigns intended to enlist the enthusiastic support of the workers without first investigating the climate of the organization. They believe they know how the employees feel about various key issues, how they perceive top management, and how they feel about belonging to the organization.

They will meet a union organizing campaign head-on, for example, completely unarmed with any evidence at all, instead of at least surveying the employees to find out how they feel. This kind of brute-force approach often backfires because the executives fail to capitalize on existing strengths and fail to identify concrete weaknesses that need to be overcome.

In fact, I have noticed over a period of years as a consultant that many executives seem to suffer from "survey-phobia" to some degree. The mere mention of an employee perception survey or a customer perception survey makes them turn pale and change the subject. Some of them will go to almost any length to avoid learning about reality. This is a short-sighted orientation, and it makes for inferior management decisions in the long run. As a general rule:

Knowing is better than not knowing.

The investigative person knows where to look for information to solve a problem, how to gather "intelligence," and how to do effective research. He or she can track down the necessary information in order to know as much as possible about the subject or problem. You have a highly tuned sense of investigative orientation when you can suspend judgment on a situation, seek out new evidence, and let the evidence guide you in your analysis.

Resistance to Enculturation

Psychologist Abraham Maslow contended that one of the most important characteristics of what he called the *self-actualizing person* is a certain degree of resistance to enculturation. By that he meant that a highly evolved person would not be entirely a product of his or her culture, but would have attitudes and values that transcended the cultural rules and norms in some cases.

The ability to resist enculturation means the ability to rely on one's own value system and sometimes to substitute one's own interpretation of a situation for the standard interpretation embraced by others. Sometimes one's approach might be in consonance with the surrounding culture, and sometimes it might be in conflict with that culture.

The radical thinkers of history who have eventually had their ideas accepted have all had this characteristic of resistance to enculturation to a high degree. Such people as Martin Luther, Mohandas Gandhi, and Martin Luther King, Jr., stood firm in their beliefs against powerful establishments, coalitions of hatred, and tremendous social pressure to abandon them. Not only did they believe as they chose, but they acted fully on their beliefs and were willing to face the consequences. The ancient Chinese philosopher Lao-tzu said, "One person who is more right than his neighbors is a majority."

Psychologists have a technical-sounding name for resistance to enculturation: they call it *critical rationality*. Ernest Hemingway had a simpler, more earthy term for it: *crap detecting*. When someone asked him what skills a writer needed to make a contribution to the ideas of his time, Hemingway snapped, "You need a good, built-in, shock-proof crap detector."

Creative thinkers have their built-in crap detectors turned on and tuned in continually. Our best social critics and commentators have excellent crap-detecting skills. Even though they irritate and unsettle many people, these critics tend to serve as the creative consciousness of the culture. People like Will Rogers and Mark Twain were skillful and merciless crap detectors. George Bernard Shaw and H. L. Mencken were also good at it, using satire, sarcasm, and wit to point out hypocrisy in the society of their times.

Don't mistake crap detecting (or critical rationality, if you prefer) for a cynical attitude or a belief that everybody is a con artist. It is a neutral, attentive attitude that lies somewhere between cynicism and gullibility. Being a good crap detector means that while you are open to new ideas, you are also alert to the possibility that someone is trying to push a special cause under the guise of something else. Crap detecting is perfectly compatible with a positive orientation, optimism, openness to new ideas, and a good sense of humor. If you are a good crap detector, you are open and receptive, but people find it very difficult to con you.

YOUR THINKING STYLE[2]

Another important aspect of thinking creatively, flexibly, and effectively is understanding your *thinking style.* Just as you have a certain style of social interaction, a style of talking, and a style of dressing, you have a style of thinking. Your thinking style is the characteristic way you process ideas. It affects the way you take in information, think about a subject, form judgments and opinions, make decisions, learn new things, and communicate with others.

Research into human brain processes has clearly shown the existence of two distinctly different modes of thought. These two modes are associated with the physical division of the brain into the left and right hemispheres. For the majority of people, the "left brain" extracts those features of the sensory data stream that are linear, sequential, symbolic, and "logical". The right brain, on the other hand, is oriented to the spatial, structural, emotional, and "intuitive" processes. These two thinking modes are so highly contrasted that you can recognize them in action by listening to the way a person talks.

Left-brain thought processes show up as statements oriented to logical reasoning, elements, sequences, facts and figures, and conceptual structures. Right-brain thought processes show up as statements about people, feelings, experiences, patterns, relations, and philosophical concepts.

A note of caution is in order in discussing brain processes. Much of what is known so far about hemispheric lateralization of the brain comes from fragmentary research and from investigations carried out with brain-damaged patients. The human brain is an enormously complex structure, and much of its activity is still only vaguely understood by researchers. Medical experts advise a great deal of caution in drawing general conclusions from what is known so far.

Nevertheless, we do know that these two contrasted modes of thought exist. Indeed, we have recognized them at least vaguely for centuries in the distinction between logical thinking and intuition. We are beginning to understand that these two thinking modes are as fundamental to the mind's operation as breathing is to the body. They are the substance of thought, so to speak.

It is also clear that most people tend to favor one of these two thinking modes over the other as they grow up and develop into adults. This tendency to rely on one predominant mode for the majority of one's thinking processes points to the concept of a cognitive style as a framework for understanding how someone thinks, learns, communicates, buys, sells, and decides. This *brain-mode preference* is one of two important dimensions of thinking style, the dimension of *structure,* or *how* a person thinks.

The other dimension of thinking style deals with *what* a person thinks, that is, the *content* of his or her thought. Here the contrast is between concrete thinking and abstract thinking. People who prefer concrete thinking tend to look for direct, tangible results. They like to deal with what is real, the here and now, and things they can experience directly. The abstract thinker, on the other hand, likes things that exist in the imagination and enjoys dealing with conceptual or theoretical subjects.

Considering thinking processes in terms of these two sets of polarities—left-brain/right-brain and concrete/abstract—gives rise to four possible combinations, or thinking styles. The four styles are:

- Left-brain concrete.
- Right-brain concrete.
- Left-brain abstract.
- Right-brain abstract.

To make these four thinking styles easy to understand and remember, I have given them metaphorical names, in terms of colors. We can call the left-brained mode of thought "blue" thinking because we tend to think of analytical people as having relatively "cool" personalities, represented by a cool color like blue. We can call the right-brained thinker a "red" thinker because we think of intuitively inclined people as having "warmer" personalities, as suggested by red.

Similarly, we can give simple metaphorical names to the other dimension—the concrete and abstract levels. We can call them "earth" and "sky" respectively. Earth thinking is concrete, immediate, and results-oriented. Sky thinking is imaginary, visual, and conceptual.

Using these metaphorical names for the four key styles, we have:

> Red Earth (right-brained concrete).
> Blue Earth (left-brained concrete).
> Red Sky (right-brained abstract).
> Blue Sky (left-brained abstract).

Figure 6–1 shows these four styles in the convenient form of a two-by-two matrix diagram.

Everybody uses all four of these thinking modes, not just one. The brain can shift from one mode to another and frequently combines them according to the demands of the task at hand. However, most people tend to have a "home base" style, one primary mode which they employ in most of their dealings with their environment. Some people are highly mobile and able to shift easily from one mode to another. Others are less mobile and have more difficulty with mode-switching. People who cannot budge from their primary thinking styles may be handicapped in some situations, not only in communicating but also in doing the kinds of thinking and problem solving that need to be done.

FIGURE 6–1: Thinking Styles

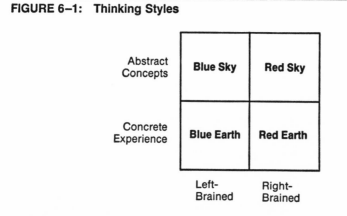

I have described each of the four basic thinking styles from the point of view of a person who favors that style very strongly. People with "combination" styles may not exhibit these tendencies so strongly as those who tend to rely heavily on a single style. The descriptions are intended to clarify the most noticeable patterns of each style and should not be construed to suggest that every person will fit neatly into only one of the four styles.

Probably the most common style is the Red Earth person, who is apt to be intuitive, people-oriented, and inclined toward direct experience. He or she tends to make decisions based on overall impressions rather than on individual facts or figures. Red Earth likes to see the outcomes of his or her efforts in concrete, tangible, recognizable form. This person has little interest in technical detail, theories, or elaborate logical processes. To the Red Earth person, feelings are "data," so to speak. His or her feelings in a situation, and the apparent feelings of others, are just as important as any other "facts". You tend to find a high proportion of Red Earth people in "people" professions like sales, social work, and counseling.

The Blue Earth is a person who values structure and order, logic, and bottom-line results. Blue Earth enjoys organizing things, solving problems logically, and doing work that involves facts, figures, and attention to detail. Fields that tend to attract Blue Earth people are accounting, certain kinds of computer programming, and some kinds of engineering.

The Red Sky is a person who likes the big picture, and is more concerned with the "what" than the "how." Red Sky tends to enjoy entrepreneurial ventures, networking with other people to accomplish big goals, and toying with global concepts and possibilities. Red Sky people tend to be drawn toward fields or activities that reward entrepreneurial thinking, but do not demand a great deal of theoretical knowledge or detail work.

The Blue Sky is the theoretician. This person values abstract ideas, logical reasoning, and relational thinking. Blue Sky also enjoys looking at the big picture, but inclines more toward organizing problems conceptually, creating theories, and working out systematic solutions. You tend to find a high proportion of Blue Sky people in fields like architecture, systems engineering, and strategic planning. The Blue Sky thinker is the one who likes to draw diagrams and models like Figure 6–1.

Again, very few people use only one of these styles to the exclusion of the others. But when a person does have a strongly dominant style, it tends to play an important part in his or her thinking processes and interactions with others. There is no "best" style. If another person with whom you are dealing does not think the same way you do, neither of you needs to be fixed. The other person is not wrong, just different. By understanding these differences and learning to adapt to them, the two of you can reach a state of "resonance," which is a highly satisfying condition of intellectual and psychological rapport.

A knowledge of thinking styles offers a number of potential benefits. It can help people communicate more skillfully. It can help people who are involved in love relationships get along more enjoyably. It equips sales people to sell more effectively. It enables managers to manage more effectively. It can help co-workers maintain positive and productive relationships. It can improve teamwork dramatically and make work more productive. And, most important, it can help you understand yourself better, appreciate the qualities that make you unique, and live with yourself more enjoyably.

A VERBAL PRESCRIPTION FOR FLEXIBILITY[3]

You can condition yourself to think more flexibly by developing semantically flexible language habits, as described previously. By requiring yourself to speak in flexible ways, you lead your brain into forming your thoughts more flexibly.

There are three simple but effective statements which you can incorporate into your regular speaking vocabulary and which have the effect of telegraphing a mentally flexible attitude to yourself as well as to others. They are:

1. I don't know.
2. I made a mistake.
3. I changed my mind.

Each of these has a special value in thinking and communication.

When you can say "I don't know" simply, nondefensively, and with a matter-of-fact tone of voice, you communicate your willingness to learn. You don't imprison your ego by pretending you know everything. You leave yourself the right to be human and the latitude to inquire.

When you can say "I made a mistake" in the same tone of voice, you acknowledge that you are human. Furthermore, you telegraph that you are openminded enough to accept a better solution. You don't get trapped in an ego-defensive situation in which you have to defend a position that doesn't make sense, even to you.

When you can say "I changed my mind" without feeling guilty or defensive, you communicate a level of confidence in your own thinking that other people tend to respect and admire. You can't be changing your mind every five minutes, of course, or as a result of every conversation you have, but it is important to be open to important new information and viewpoints.

Actually, each of these flexibility cues is a form of self-assertion. By using these statements judiciously in your conversation with others, you claim your right to be human. You stay out of ego traps, and you also help yourself stay saner by maintaining a realistic, reality-based frame of mind.

NOTES

[1] The information in this section comes from *Mindex: Your Thinking Style Profile*™, © Dr. Karl Albrecht (San Diego: Shamrock Press, 1983). All rights reserved. Used by permission.

[2] Ibid.

[3] For more information on mental flexibility, see Karl Albrecht, *Brain Power: Learn to Develop Your Thinking Skills* (Englewood Cliffs, N.J.: Prentice-Hall, 1980).

Divergent Thinking and Convergent Thinking

"The important thing is not to stop questioning."

ALBERT EINSTEIN

Psychologists recognize two distinctly different kinds of thought processes associated with problem solving: *divergent thinking* and *convergent thinking.* Every decision you ever make, every problem you come to grips with, large or small, significant or insignificant, involves these two thinking processes.

Your brain goes through the same kinds of activity when you solve the problem of what to do for lunch as when you solve the problem of what to do about your career, a major project, or the direction of an entire company. The content of your thought will be radically different in these different situations, but the process will be much the same.

In any decision you must first think about the various facts, issues, constraints, and options involved. This is the first phase of your thought process; if you do it well, the second phase will be more effective.

The second phase, after you have considered the ins and outs of the problem situation, starts when you zero in on a course of action. You make your decision, choose the option you want, and abandon the others. Your mind goes into a very different state during this phase.

The first stage of your thought process is the divergent thinking or *expansion* phase. The second stage is the convergent thinking or *closure* phase. This may seem like a fairly mundane, straightforward distinction, but I urge you not to pass over it too lightly. It is one of the most important concepts in the entire subject of creative thinking. It is the key to the ability to solve problems and make decisions effectively.

To get more comfortable with the concept of divergent and convergent thinking, consider the implications of the terms themselves. To diverge means to expand, to spread out, to reach out. To converge means to contract, to close in, to come to a single point. Both are valuable to your thinking processes. Each has its advantages at various points in the problem-solving chain of events. In any problem-solving situation you first start with a broad consideration of the factors and choices involved (divergent thinking), and second, you follow through with the final decision-making process, which is deciding what you'll actually do (convergent thinking).

These thought processes differ in the manner in which your brain handles the information that forms the subject matter of the problem. Divergent thinking consists of expanding the picture of the problem. It involves stating the problem in various forms, turning it over and looking at it from various points of view, questioning and requestioning basic facts and opinions, identifying values and key factors, gathering more facts and ideas, and generating various options for solving it. Divergent thinking is expansive—it creates a bigger and bigger picture, to make sure you understand the problem well before you proceed to make the choices available to you.

Divergent thinking is not a matter of having any one idea. Rather it is the *progression* of ideas in your mind when you are going from the specific to the general, from the narrow to the broad, and from the concrete to the conceptual. When you're generating options rather than choosing among them, that's divergent thinking. Think of divergent thought as "split-apart" thinking, spreading and expanding outwardly.

Convergent thinking operates in just the reverse way. It narrows down the problem to a smaller, more manageable size and perspective. It casts out various options in favor of a preferred few. It zeroes in on selected key factors, magnifies them, analyzes them, and evaluates the options to prepare the way to make the choices. Convergent thinking is reductive; it settles on a smaller and more detailed picture to prepare us for action.

Convergent thinking is the progression of ideas in your mind when you're leaving generalizations behind and going to the specifics, from the broad to the narrow, from the conceptual to the concrete, and from the many to the few. When you're choosing one option among many, you are thinking convergently. Whereas divergent ideas fly apart, convergent ideas come together. Convergent thinking is focused, specific, and targeted. It is much more concentrated and narrowly focused than is divergent thinking. Convergent thinking is reductive and more likely to involve logical conclusions.

MAKING DECISIONS

Let's take a slow-motion look at a very mundane problem-solving process and see how both modes of thinking play a part. Let's examine the simple act of deciding where to go for lunch. In the divergent phase, you ask yourself a series of questions and consider various options. Do you want to eat at your desk, at a fast-food restaurant, or at a nice, quiet restaurant? Do you want to eat alone or go with someone? Should you invite your boss? How much time do you have? Are you willing to drive, or do you want to go somewhere within walking distance? What would you like to eat? Which is more important: good food, atmosphere, or speed and convenience? All of this mental process, even if it only takes two or three seconds, is divergent thinking.

You begin to think convergently when you make your final decisions. You converge when you pick a restaurant, for instance. Then you get in the car with your friend, drive to the place, and find a table. Now you look at the menu and you must think divergently again. What do you want to order? Should you eat lightly because you have a big date tonight, or should you have a substantial meal because you plan to work late? Which items on the menu are your favorites? Is price a factor? Do you want to split something with the person you're having lunch with?

A workday luncheon with a friend may seem like a trivial decision-making process and may not warrant much conscious thought. You probably don't want to get out your pen and paper and analyze the decision in great detail. *Low-consequence decisions* like lunch don't usually need much divergent thinking.

On the other hand, what if this particular lunch is important to your career? Maybe you're having lunch with your boss to discuss your upcoming promotion. Or maybe it's with an important customer or client. In that case it might make sense to do a considerable amount of divergent processing of the issue. You might want to select a restaurant very carefully for a meeting in which you and others will be negotiating an important deal. You might want a restaurant where you're sure you and your client won't have to sit and wait for 30 minutes for a table. You might want a place that offers privacy, so there is no risk of being over-heard by potential competitors.

All during this decision-making process, divergent and convergent thinking are going on rapidly, even in your unconscious mind. You are choosing options, weighing alternatives, and finally making decisions. How do you think while making a critical decision concerning your career? Presumably, that involves far greater analysis on your part. Unlike a casual lunch, this is not a choice you make in 30 seconds. You begin to think divergently when you ask yourself if you want to switch to another company, start your own business, or change careers entirely. During the divergent process you are gathering facts and information and turning things over in your mind until you switch to a convergent mode, where you actually make your choice. This may require months, rather than seconds, and it will usually be a very conscious process.

One of the keys to being effective in decision-making situations is knowing which problems warrant extensive thought and which ones don't really count that much. In any business situation, the real purpose of divergent thinking is to help you converge more effectively. You need to know how to use both processes to be a good problem solver.

You Need a "Zoom Lens"

Let me use the experience of taking a picture with a camera as an analogy to help put divergent and convergent thinking into a more concrete frame of reference. Divergent thinking is a lot like having a wide-angle lens on your camera. It gathers many different things into one scene. If you want to get all of Westminster Abbey in your picture, you need that wide-angle shot. Divergent thinking works the same way. It sees more than just one aspect; it sees a multitude of aspects.

Convergent thinking is a lot like having a narrow-angle tele-photo lens on your camera. It focuses in on one specific thing. If you want to get a picture of the detail work on the roof of the Sydney Opera House, you need a close-up shot. That's the way convergent thinking works. It sees one feature close up; it magnifies one aspect of the problem. Both lenses are useful under certain circumstances and in specific situations. To take good pictures, you need a wide-angle lens and a telephoto lens, not just one or the other.

But now suppose your camera has a zoom lens, which allows you to adjust the angle of view. You can take the whole scene or just a selected part of it. By adjusting your zoom lens, you can widen the angle of the picture to take in the entire Golden Gate Bridge, and you can zoom in to pick out the details of the structure or the suspension cables.

The zoom lens now represents both divergent and convergent thinking in combination. When you can shift back and forth between the divergent process and the convergent process, you have, in effect, a zoom lens for your mind.

The most effective and creative thinkers have this zoom lens capability as a matter of habit. They can think divergently when necessary and convergently when necessary. Another very important characteristic of the creative mind is that its zoom lens is set for wide angle much of the time. In other words, creative people tend to react divergently rather than convergently to the new, the odd, and the unusual. They have a bias toward diverging at the first instant of perception. They realize that it's easier for the mind to zoom in than it is for it to zoom out. That is, it's easier to converge than it is to diverge. Therefore, they try to take a wide-angle snapshot of the situation first, and zoom in from there.

Let's Make It Really Tough

The real test of your ability to think flexibly and creatively comes in a situation that involves conflict, strong feelings, or a strongly held position on both sides. Just about anybody can apply the techniques of creative thinking in a classroom case study dealing with the problem of improving the education of children or finding a way to save costs in manufacturing. The going gets much tougher when feelings run high, stakes are high, and people aren't in the mood to think creatively. Let's use an example of an actual conflict situation with real physical dangers in it.

Police officials in a large city meet to discuss the question of how to handle a large upcoming antipolice rally in a minority neighborhood. The gathering will probably draw together some of the most angry and hostile members of the community. Even though it is an antipolice rally, the police must provide some degree of security and supervision, just as they would for any other large public gathering. The police planners must decide how to supervise the rally and what, if any, kind of proactive or reactive stance to take.

The meeting comes to order with a dozen ranking and non-ranking personnel in attendance. The scope of the problem is introduced: What is the best way for us to deal with this rally? As the discussion progresses, one of the patrol officers in the group throws out a really off-the-wall suggestion. "What if we went to the rally unarmed? Just wearing our uniforms and badges, with no guns, as a show of good faith?" What follows after that suggestion is an example of divergers and convergers at work in their respective "comfort zones."

The convergers in the group—seeking to "close" the issue—immediately begin to protest vehemently that the idea is ridiculous. No cop in his or her right mind would go to this rally without a gun for protection. The convergent thinkers immediately reject the idea and attempt to move on.

The divergers in the group take a different attitude. They listen impassively to the proposal and sit back to think about the ramifications. Without passing judgment, the divergent thinkers look at the options and discuss the possibilities with the rest of the group members. Meanwhile, the convergent thinkers have rejected the idea and are now attempting to drive the divergers into submission.

Obviously, the conflict raised in this question is a matter of great significance. The idea of the police going to an antipolice rally without their weapons is a very unorthodox and far-out proposition. But a divergent examination of the problem will give them a better idea of the options available for consideration. The members of the discussion group are experts in their field and they have their own opinions as to the validity of the suggestion.

How would you decide, if the situation were placed in your hands? Would you view the problem divergently, by exploring the alternatives, or would you think convergently and try to decide the question with a snap judgment? To paraphrase a familiar statement:

It isn't what you decide to do, but how you decide to do it that counts.

THE BEST OF BOTH WORLDS

The key to being a skilled problem solver is to be able to combine both modes, the divergent and the convergent, and to use them appropriately according to the needs of the situation. By being able to shift your thought processes from wide angle to telephoto consciously and easily, you can be highly flexible in your grasp of the problem.

Unfortunately, it seems to be much easier for the human mind to think convergently than divergently. The vast majority of people are thoroughly conditioned to respond convergently at the instant of perception of a new, unusual, or unfamiliar idea. They are habitual convergers. This can be an asset when the problem that presents itself is simple and straightforward. But when it involves a number of confusion factors, conflicting objectives, and complicated constraints, the convergent thinker gets frustrated.

Relatively few people are skilled at both divergent and convergent thinking. Most tend to rely on one more than the other. If a person is a habitual diverger, and is not willing or able to converge when necessary, he or she tends to be "out in the ozone" much of the time. This person comes across as "flaky" to people who are convergers.

Conversely, the habitual converger may jump to conclusions and make snap decisions without adequately exploring the various ramifications of the problem. This person may have such a rigidly developed habit of narrowing every issue down to simple terms and lunging immediately for familiar solutions that he or she cannot easily produce new ideas or adopt new or novel points of view. We describe this person as narrow-minded.

Think about your own habitual reaction patterns. How do you react at the instant you see or hear something new or different?

Can you react divergently at first, seeing the possibilities in the idea? Can you defer your value judgments and reserve them until you have had time to consider the idea? Or do you react convergently, evaluating it in a split second? How do you rate as a thinker? Are you overly divergent or overly convergent? Can you use both styles of thought effectively? How do other people see you? Do people look to you for ideas? Are you an idea killer? Or do you help people with their ideas? An honest appraisal of your thinking habits may be one of the most important things for you to think about. In other words, think about how you think.

If your answers to some of these questions trouble you, then it may be time to change some of your habitual patterns of thought.

DO DECISIONS HAVE TO BE DEMOCRATIC?

If you are a manager or if you work in any leadership role with other people, you may need to be conscious of your decision-making habits. Many managers tend to feel guilty or confused about the way they make decisions. So-called participative management theories tell you to seek and accept feedback from your staff. It is supposed to be an open, collaborative process that will help you make easier decisions because of the many options offered by your co-workers.

Even though it is important to be flexible in your thinking processes, that is, to have your zoom lens in the wide-angle mode much of the time, that doesn't mean that your decisions are not your own. Listening to the viewpoints of others can help you make high-quality decisions, but it doesn't obligate you to decide in their favor. No matter how many people have given you their advice and comments, if you are the leader, the final decision is still up to you.

If you are a manager, there are times when you must proceed on the basis of your own judgment, even if other people in your organization think you are wrong. You mustn't be afraid to take the steps you believe you need to take.

When John F. Kennedy was president, he tended to call upon the views of others to a great extent, but he didn't hesitate to decide an issue in his own way. On one occasion Kennedy was having a meeting with his cabinet in his White House office. He put forth an idea for a certain program which met with a very lukewarm response from his cabinet members. The more the president tried to convince his cabinet of the merits of his idea, the less progress he made.

Finally, Kennedy put the issue to a vote. He asked for a show of hands in favor of the proposal. Except for himself, no one in the room raised his hand in agreement. He then asked for a show of hands voting against the idea. Every hand in the room shot up in the air. But Kennedy was determined to have it his way on this particular issue. He looked around at his cabinet members and said with a wry smile, "Well, gentlemen, it looks like the 'ayes' have it."

TYPE "A" DECISIONS AND TYPE "B" DECISIONS

Actually, Kennedy's only sin was misleading his advisers about his decision-making process on this particular issue. He had led them to believe it was going to be a collaborative decision. They thought he wanted the benefit of their knowledge and their views. In fact, he really wanted them to ratify a decision he had already made in his mind.

One executive I worked for many years ago observed, after he had failed to persuade us to adopt his idea, "Well, the only difference between rape and seduction is salesmanship. I see I haven't sold you, so I'm going to direct you to do it." This kind of decision-making pattern tends to confuse people and make them resentful. It makes no sense to tell them you want their ideas and opinions when you have no intention of listening to them at all.

On the other hand, there is no law of the universe that says a manager is obligated to confer with the people in his or her unit on every issue. In this era of "one-minute managing" and "management by walking around," some managers feel guilty if they don't allow people to participate in the decision-making process. They think that somehow morale will go down or people's feelings will be hurt. Some other managers take the opposite tack and say, "I make the decisions around here. I know what's going on, I'm the one who's responsible, and I don't work by democracy." It seems to me that both points of view are unnecessarily narrow and counterproductive.

I have seen so much confusion and uncertainty among managers on this one point over the years that I finally developed an explicit policy about it, which I recommend to all managers. At your next staff meeting, bring up the subject of decision making in your organization. Tell the people the following thing. "There are two types of decisions I make around here. Let's call them Type A and Type B decisions. On any particular issue that comes up, I'll tell you whether I plan to deal with it as an A decision or a B decision."

An A decision is one that is collaborative. In an A decision situation, you ask for as much help and advice as you can get from your employees. You are still the one who is responsible for making the decision, of course, but you want to base it on the best information, ideas, and points of view you can get from the people on your team.

A B decision is noncollaborative. You are not interested, nor will you listen to any input concerning a B decision. You take sole ownership of the decision, and you have no particular intention of consulting with anybody else about it. Others may not like the idea of your reserving the decision for yourself, but you let them know that all resistance is futile. It will be your decision, and that is that. They can turn their minds to other things.

What you are doing is *deciding how you will decide*, which is a fairly sophisticated way of approaching the situation. The important thing is letting the staff know which decisions you have reserved as B decisions and which qualify as A decisions. If you tell them you are open to hearing their views on a certain matter, but you have already made up your mind, they will smoke you out right away. They will know that you are not really going to listen to what they say. This kind of treatment by a manager makes people resentful, cynical, and scornful of the manager's style of dealing with people. It quickly extinguishes their enthusiasm and sense of involvement. They resort to just doing their jobs and asking the manager what he or she wants to do on each issue.

Conversely, people usually feel so good about having an opportunity to take part in solving an important problem that their participation in the thinking process is in itself a kind of reward.

They feel a sense of involvement, empowerment, and pride in participating. They feel an important social and intellectual bond with the leader. They are much more likely to put their energies into their work because they believe that what they think and what they have to say really counts for something.

You have no obligation to make all of your decisions A decisions. On the other hand, if virtually all of your important decisions are B decisions, you need to ask yourself whether you are making the best use of the resources available to you. Two or more heads *are* often better than one.

CHAPTER EIGHT

How to Become an Idea Machine

"The purpose of your body is to carry your brain around."

THOMAS EDISON

Did you ever notice that some people never seem to run out of ideas? These people are always thinking and constantly coming up with new ways to do things. They can see five or six immediate solutions instead of just one. Some people have a creative drive that lets them generate one idea after another, just like a machine.

Many of our greatest inventors were idea machines—people who could create hundreds of ideas in a short period of time. Henry Ford's automobile assembly line, Edison's light bulb, and the Wright Brothers' airplane all came from people who could create and follow through with not only one idea but a multitude of them.

How does this process occur? What makes an idea machine tick? There are certain processes that you as a creative person can follow to generate ideas. You can teach yourself to become an idea producer. These idea-production skills can help you solve problems, create new options, or just think of a way to do something you've never done before.

In the beginning stages of solving a problem by using idea production, it's better to think about the quantity of your ideas rather than the quality. People who are idea machines don't spend their time evaluating their ideas when they first have them; there's time for that later. If you take too much time to evaluate your ideas as they appear, you could end up talking yourself out of the ideas. You also tend to waste time deciding, when you could be thinking of other alternatives. Learn to mass-produce your ideas first and think about their validity later.

There are a number of ways to help you keep track of your ideas. The easiest one involves only an ink pen. You should learn to carry a pen with you at all times and to use it to put your ideas down on paper for later study. How many times have you thought of a brilliant idea and later couldn't remember it because you didn't write it down? Get used to putting your thoughts on paper while they are still fresh in your mind.

Being an idea machine can have positive benefits for your personal and career goals. Let's use an example of how an idea-machine thinker can help out in the organizational environment.

One of the hallmarks of creative thinkers in a corporation is their ability to generate ideas on a continual basis and also think up ideas in a timely fashion. These thinkers can crank out ideas at will, instead of only when a crash project or a group effort calls for idea production skills.

These innovative people know their ideas can often affect the entire company, not just their particular department. So they know how to come up with the most feasible ideas within a short period of time. Creative thinking in the corporation means meeting the demands of the organization in a timely manner. Good ideas that arrive too late to solve a problem are of no value to the company. Creative thinkers know how to generate ideas quickly and can "think on their feet" when necessary.

BE AN OPTION THINKER

People we refer to as idea machines can often find new angles to solve a particular problem. They are not always satisfied with one single solution or any one idea. They don't leap at the first seemingly right solution and are not afraid to give the problem further study. Some people working in a group environment like to jump on the bandwagon and accept the first feasible idea, just to end the discussion. The creative option thinker doesn't put time limits on creativity. He or she is not afraid to fully discuss the problem and analyze all of the available options. This is a worthwhile trait in the organizational setting as it can help draw out many solutions not thought of before. It also improves the synergy of the group.

Idea producers solve problems in terms of options that work for them. While it is important to generate a large number of ideas to solve a problem, it is also important to recognize the *right* solution as well. Many people can generate ideas, but not everyone can generate a large number of workable ideas.

Some people spend too much time holding onto an idea that won't work for one reason or another. The trick is to discover the best ideas as a solution to your problem. It is far easier to make a difficult decision when you have a number of options to pick from. You shouldn't be overly critical of your ideas as they come. You must, however, learn to differentiate between ideas that aren't feasible and ideas that will work for you.

APPRECIATE NOVELTY

One day the artist Pablo Picasso was standing outside his house looking around the yard. His eyes fell upon a rusty old bicycle near the porch. As he looked at the metal frame of the bike, he noticed that the handlebars resembled the horns of a bull. He removed the handlebars from the bike, went back into his studio, and created a sculpture of a charging bull. Picasso used his creative imagination to make something dramatic out of something seemingly ordinary. He did not limit himself or his creative ideas to any one specific theme.

Creative thinkers are always on the lookout for new ideas. They see novel ways to approach a specific problem and can use their creativity to find a new solution, using an unrelated idea if it fits. While this appreciation for a novel idea might attract criticism from peers, creative thinkers know that novel ideas often solve complex problems. They are not held back by the negative opinions of their co-workers, peers, or associates.

JUMP THE TRACK

One of the ways to remain open to other options and ideas is to be flexible in your thinking. This flexibility lets you "jump the track" from one train of thought to another more feasible one.

In his classic creativity book *Lateral Thinking*, Edward de Bono explains the differences between so-called vertical thinking and lateral thinking:

> Lateral thinking is quite distinct from vertical thinking, which is the traditional type of thinking. In vertical thinking one moves forward by sequential steps, each of which must be justified. The distinction between the two types of thinking is sharp. For instance, in lateral thinking one uses information not for its own sake but for its effect. In lateral thinking one may have to be wrong at some stage in order to achieve a correct solution; in vertical thinking this would be impossible.[1]

Here de Bono is saying that his lateral thinking allows you to be wrong and still be able to discover a solution. This lies in your ability to change directions after your mistakes and still solve the problem. "Vertical thinking," says de Bono, "is selective. Lateral thinking is generative."

De Bono also makes the distinction that people who are good idea machines are also skilled at lateral thinking:

> Lateral thinking is closely related to creativity. But whereas creativity is too often only the description of a result, lateral thinking is the description of a process. One can only admire a result but one can learn to use a process.
>
> Lateral thinking is concerned with the generation of new ideas. New ideas are the stuff of change and progress in every field from science to art, from politics to personal happiness.[2]

His term *lateral thinking* is now such a common phrase in the discussion of human creativity and thought that the Oxford Dictionary gives it a place as one of the statements that have become part of our language.

APPRECIATE HUMOR

Most of us enjoy the humor of good comedians like Bill Cosby, George Carlin, and Woody Allen. These people have divergent thinking styles and their minds are quite creative. They can generate a tremendous number of creatively funny ideas solely on the basis of what they witness around them. Humor itself is very creative, innovative, and thought-provoking.

Bill Cosby, as an example, derives his humor from the seemingly ordinary events that originated with his childhood and his family. With Cosby's flair for the outrageous, he can make us laugh with the verbal portraits he paints of these events. We have all experienced some of the same humorous episodes of family life. Cosby's creative talents lie in his ability to exploit these situations.

George Carlin's humor exploits commonplace items in our society and in our homes. He refers to many of his questions about life as his "mental hotfoots." One of them includes the seemingly innocuous statement, "Why are there no blue foods?" Carlin's flair for the outrageous, his critical social perceptions, and his frequent use of hyperbole make him an effective comedian.

Much of Woody Allen's humor lies in his ability to denigrate himself by using the stereotypes and prejudices of our society. He is often a sharp social critic, but his satire is carefully masked by his humor. His perceptions of life are based on his observations of how human beings mistreat one another. Yet his humor is displayed in a humorous and imaginative manner.

All three of these men earn their living making us laugh. They exploit a common situation and exaggerate the outcome so much that we find them very funny. They have developed certain routines that comment on the irony, hypocrisy, and idiocy of our world. You could refer to this as developing "mutations" of the realities in our society. It is their innovative thinking skills that make them so effective at their work. They are careful social observers who choose to comment on what they see by using humor. Humor, especially social satire, is often a watchdog of our times.

The idea producer also learns to utilize a version of this exploitation and flair for the hyperbolic. Creative business ideas often arise from a defined social need.

PUT YOUR JUDGMENT ON HOLD

One way to make it easier to come up with new ideas is to teach yourself to suspend your judgment. Deciding too early about one of your ideas is not good for the overall health of the idea. Wait until you have all the information you need before you begin to whittle away at the idea.

Making abrupt judgments about ideas is often the role of the idea killer, who likes to make quick and often harsh judgments when someone proposes a new idea. You can avoid this destructive habit by improving your listening skills. When you are talking with someone, let that person finish before you evaluate his or her response. The best way to properly evaluate an idea is to have all the facts at hand before you make any judgment. Even if you vehemently disagree with the opinion of the other person, wait until he or she is done before you give your point of view. After all, it's only fair, and you expect the same standard of treatment from the other individual.

When you are discussing something with someone, ask that person for his or her point of view instead of his or her position. Ask that person to back up that point of view with facts, not just opinions. Try to elicit the most factual information you can before you decide. Try not to prejudice yourself with preconceived opinions about the subject matter.

CHANGING YOUR OUTLOOK

You can build a better mousetrap, so to speak, by thinking creatively and producing and developing your ideas. Look for the novelty in things that you come across. Even the most simple of objects can be used in a hundred different ways. Remember that Thomas Edison tried over 700 different materials before he found the right metals to make a filament for his light bulb. He showed his unique ability to mass-produce ideas, his investigative orientation, and his tolerance for an ambiguous situation all at once.

Look for combinations in things. See how certain objects work in harmony with each other and how certain ones don't. Look for seemingly disparate ideas that actually form workable combinations. The important thing in producing ideas is to be flexible. Nobody ever became an idea machine by sticking to the tried-and-true path all of the time. Like innovative thinkers, idea producers are not afraid to buck the status quo from time to time. Innovative and creative ideas often come from people who produce the most ideas. While it is true that problems are occasionally solved via the "cosmic ray of inspiration," this is not usually the case. Idea producers have solved seemingly complex problems only after they considered a myriad of other options before deciding on their final choice.

PRODUCE, PRODUCE, PRODUCE!

The whole basis of becoming an idea machine is the mass production of ideas. One metaphor to help you with this distinction is to treat the concept of idea production like popcorn production. You put the popcorn in the pan, add oil, and heat it. When the kernels reach a certain temperature, they pop. Idea production is very similar. Creativity lays the groundwork for idea production. Ideas spring into your mind like popcorn, under the right circumstances. These circumstances include: a positive frame of mind, a sense of humor, an appreciation for novelty, and a tolerance for ambiguity. I've discussed many of these factors throughout Part Two—A Crash Course in Creativity.

DO MENTAL CALISTHENICS

Many creative thinkers frequently use the well-known concept of brainstorming as an idea production technique. You can take it a little further by using an example of a brainstorming exercise. Let's do some mental calisthenics and go through an idea production exercise.

Take a common office object like a paper clip, and think of what you could use it for besides holding paper together. Stop reading at this point and get a paper clip. When you have one, take a pen and paper and begin to brainstorm. If you'll recall, brainstorming means free-associating your ideas, writing them down without judging them, and generating as many options as you possibly can. Stop reading and make up your list. When you've exhausted all of the possibilities, come back and compare it to the one in this book.

A lock pick.
A fingernail cleaner.
A fishhook.
A safety pin.
A tie clip.

A tool to change the time on your digital watch.
A key ring.
A screwdriver.
A temporary button.
A scratching tool.
A toothpick.
A temporary fuse.
A wire.
An earring.

How did you fare? Did you come up with some of the same ideas? Did you think of others? If you came up with more than these, you can classify yourself as a creative thinker. Don't be discouraged if you had a little trouble coming up with more than a few options. This exercise helps improve your idea production and brainstorming skills. See if you can use this exercise to come up with new uses for other common office or household items.

This idea generation technique teaches you the skill of option thinking. If you can think of a number of different uses for a common paper clip, think about how many options you may be able to think of when you tackle a specific management or organizational problem.

CREATIVE DOODLING

Everyone knows how to doodle. Doodling is defined as *drawing or scribbling idly,* but it is much more than that. Doodling is often idea production in its raw form. Sit at your desk or in a restaurant and doodle on your scratch pad or a convenient placemat. Your creativity is wide open at this point, as you toy with a concept or the design for some new product you're thinking about. Doodling does not have to be limited to cartoonlike pictures alone. Often doodling allows you to mass-produce ideas in a relatively unstructured fashion. There are no hard-and-fast rules for doodling. It is a powerful yet rarely used form of idea production.

Doodles can even be a list of words that relate to a concept you wish to develop. They can be sketches, diagrams, or charts and graphs. Any of these formats can trigger an idea for you. The subject of doodling brings up the importance of having a pen or a pencil with you at all times. You'd be amazed at the number of people who don't even carry a simple ballpoint pen. A pen is a powerful creative thinking tool. You can use it to scratch a note anytime a creative urge strikes you: waiting in a checkout line, sitting in traffic, or eating a meal are all times when an idea may occur to you that you'll want to write down. Having a pen and a piece of paper will keep you from losing a potentially powerful idea. Plan for your creative ideas to come at seemingly inopportune moments. Realize how valuable a pen can be to help you become an idea machine.

Another way to generate creative ideas is to keep an idea list. This can be as simple as having a notepad by your desk, or as sophisticated as using a microcomputer and an idea-organizing software package to set up a database of ideas. Write down every idea you have, no matter how insignificant it may seem at the time of creation. An idea list lets you capture your thoughts on paper and preserves them for further study at another time.

It is important to list your ideas while they are still fresh in your mind. How many times does the phone ring and distract you while some major project is under way? An idea list saves your most important and creative thoughts. Studies have shown that few people remember a fleeting idea after dealing with an unrelated or distracting topic. It may seem like oversimplification, but seeing your thoughts on paper can go a long way toward improving your creative problem-solving ability. Encourage your co-workers to keep their own idea lists. These lists can trigger creative thinking and give everyone some excellent discussion topics for committee meetings and group participation exercises.

Make sure your supervisor knows that you keep an idea list. If a specific problem arises within the organization, he or she will know that you may have a list of possible solutions or options and may call on you to provide an answer. The idea list is a very powerful tool to help you think creatively. It doesn't have to be a large production, just a few notes jotted on a pad as a way of reminding you of certain ideas and also reinforcing your creativity skills. As new problems occur in your organization, try to add new ideas and possible solutions to your list each day.

Learn to appreciate your ideas, no matter how small or insignificant they may appear to be at the time. Not every idea you have will solve the world peace problem or lower the national debt, but who is to say that it perhaps won't? Creative thinkers are constantly on the lookout for possible solutions to problems using their own creative options. Sometimes the most offbeat idea is the one that solves the problem. Appreciate the novelty and creativity of your ideas. After all, they come from you and they are *your* ideas.

THE VALUE OF YOUR IDEAS

In an upcoming chapter I will talk at length about idea killers. I'm sure you've met this kind of person frequently. These are the people who murder creative, innovative thoughts before they reach the actual development stage. The idea killer can judge and dismiss an idea before it has had its chance to bloom. Many companies are filled with idea killers, who lurk in committee meetings and staff conferences. These people can do vast amounts of harm to the budding creative thinkers in the company. In effect, they "steal" and destroy a valuable resource from the organization—its creativity. If you allow the idea killer to roam freely, you run the risk of losing this precious and sensitive asset from the members of the firm.

My final point about becoming an idea machine is that all of your ideas should have a certain intrinsic value, if not to the idea killer, then to you. Learn to appreciate your creativity. Don't be too judgmental about your own (or anybody else's) form of creativity. We all think differently and we all see things from a different point of view. All ideas have merit, even though the value or feasibility of a new idea may not be obvious at first. Learn to nurture your ideas and the ideas of other people as you hear them. Offer your support to other people's new ideas. They may lack the speaking and selling skills needed to take an idea from the development stage to the final implementation stage. Your ideas add to your own intellectual wealth and define you as a creative, innovative individual in the organization.

The best idea producers are not always the most skilled idea sellers. If you fall into that category, the trick is to improve your communication skills so you can persuade other people to see the creativity of your ideas. You need to develop your articulation skills so you can convince others of the importance and success of your ideas. You must have the flexibility to hear and accept the ideas of others, without prejudgment. Once you have heard and reviewed the ideas of other people, you can build on their creativity by adding to the depth and scope of their original thoughts. An effective idea producer is not afraid to expand the ideas of others. This does not mean you should go around taking credit for the innovation of others, only that you are able to build a foundation on their creativity. Remember that your efforts as an idea producer and creator are for the good of the whole organization, as well as for your specific department.

In a group or committee setting, you needn't consider the production of ideas to be a race among thinkers. Idea production should benefit everyone in the company. Option thinking and creative thought in general should not be limited to only a few innovative thinkers in a company. It is a mistake to relegate the innovative thinking duties to the research and development department when the sales or production departments may have their own creative innovations to share. Potentially, everyone can be involved in the idea production process. It is your responsibility to improve your idea production skills for the good of your organization and especially for your own personal well-being. If you enhance your role as a powerful thinker, people within the organization will look to you for help. Take every advantage you can to display and develop your creativity. We know idea machines are creative, innovative, and positive thinkers. So start being your own idea machine.

NOTES

[1]Edward de Bono, *Lateral Thinking* (New York: Harper & Row, 1970), pp. 11–12.

[2]Ibid.

Positive Thinking

"There is nothing sadder than a young pessimist."

MARK TWAIN

Creative, innovative thinkers have a distinct orientation toward the positive side of things. They have a bias in favor of optimism, positive expectations, and a belief in themselves, all flavored with a sense of humor. The creative, innovative thinker starts, persists, and finishes with a positive slant to his or her thinking. This person makes a habit of seeing the wine bottle as half full rather than half empty, and likely to be full again in the future.

So much has been written about positive thinking, and there are so many commonplace expressions in our language about it, that you would think that positive thinking is something everybody knows about and practices. Yet the evidence of everyday life makes it abundantly clear that relatively few people really know how to keep their thoughts on a positive plane most of the time. More people talk about positive thinking than practice it.

There is so much preoccupation in the media and in our day-to-day lives with failure, disaster, and fear, that a large majority of people go about their lives with a negative tinge to their consciousness. This negative bias brought about by all of this fear-based subject matter leads to a negative bias in their emotional status. Very few people consciously realize that they are the ones in charge of their current mental state and their feelings.

How do you know when you're thinking positively? Very simple: you feel good. Positive thinking is the kind of thinking that you're doing when your emotions are positive and you feel good about yourself. Working backward from that definition, the skill of positive thinking is just putting your mind on subject matter that produces the result of feeling good.

THE MEDIA ENVIRONMENT: PACKAGED FEAR

Americans, more than the people of any other country in the world, live in an environment of *synthetic information*. We have more information coming at us at a faster rate than anyone else. It's coming at us from all sides. We get images of our country and the world from radio, television, magazines, newspapers, and movies. It can be startling when you realize that only a small part of the library of "experience images" you carry around in your head have come from your own personal experience. Most of them come from electronic, photographic, or verbal reports from others who bring you programs and the news.

People who live in remote corners of the world, say, Bali or Tibet or the Amazon jungles, have to rely almost solely on their own eyes and ears to form their concept of the world. Direct personal experience plus the effects of a small number of verbal reports from others form the totality of their knowledge of their world.

Those of us who live in more technologically advanced societies have the benefit of a tremendous tide of external imagery. We can vicariously experience scenes and happenings all over the world. In a matter of days or weeks, we can "experience" things which the more primitive person could never hope to experience in a lifetime.

Unfortunately, there is a profoundly important bias to the information we experience through the media. The vast majority of it has been *chosen* for its emotional impact by those who gather and transmit it. It costs money to gather and transmit images, and they must have market value for the media companies to be interested in them.

Pick up a typical daily newspaper and what do you see? The headlines usually speak of crisis, conflict, and disaster much more often than of progress, harmony and success. The latest terrorist bombing or natural disaster that killed thousands of people sells papers. Apparently, progress and prosperity are boring products for the information market. When was the last time you saw a headline that read, "Nothing Bad Happened Today, People Were Nice to Each Other"?

The television environment is much the same, but doubled in spades. Television news is often filled with negative stories, which are accompanied by equally negative pictures of these events. The negativity pervading the shows people watch strongly influences their thoughts and feelings.

I have no particular sermon to preach about the media, but I do believe we as individuals are responsible to ourselves for the kinds of information we bring into our mental computers. Computer people have an old expression: GIGO, or "Garbage In, Garbage Out." If you put mental and emotional garbage into your computer, that is what it processes. And that is what it tends to produce. But if you give it positive inputs, positive images, positive experiences, positive ideas, and positive feedback, it will tend to produce positive outputs.

THE POWER OF POSITIVE THOUGHT

Many people pay lip service to the phrase *positive thinking*. It is a term used in sales meetings, touchy-feely self-help books, and motivational seminars. It is not often linked with creative thought, however. The connection between the two characteristics stems from the way you adjust your own attitude. How many creative thoughts did you have the last time you were in a bad mood? Probably not very many. Negative feelings stifle creative ideas.

Think of how creative and innovative you feel when you come to the office in a good mood. Your work load seems more manageable, and you often can't wait to tackle the problems of the day. You feel like turning on your creative skills and going after old problems in new ways. This attitude can go a long way toward making you more productive.

If you want to know if people are willing to think positively in a group or a meeting, start by asking them how they feel. Notice that the ones who gripe and complain about their workload or other problems within the organization contribute the least in the way of creative ideas to the discussion. These complainers are often also the idea killers of the company. Their negative feelings and low self-worth inhibit their own creativity. Unfortunately, because they don't see themselves as creative thinkers, they may tend to stifle the creativity of other people as well. They are quick to shoot down a valuable idea in its early stages.

People who generally feel positive, energetic, and happy contribute the most creative and innovative ideas to any discussion.

Positive thinking is a frame of mind that you can enhance and develop. This positive frame of mind is an important step toward stimulating your own creativity.

TALK POSITIVELY AND YOU'LL THINK POSITIVELY

You can find one of the clearest cues about your ability to think positively in your language habits. What you say and how you say it is linked to how you feel when you speak. Negative people talk negatively. Their routine conversation is laden with critical, pessimistic, discouraging, fear-oriented speech patterns.

Most people are familiar with Murphy's Law: "If anything can go wrong, it will." It is a trite phrase that has been around for years. Posters, greeting cards, and notepads all display Murphy's Law in one form or another. Even though it has a humorous ring to it when you first hear it, Murphy's Law is a cynical construct of the defeatist mind. It projects a highly negative point of view that can color your expectations and lead you to accept defeat and failure unnecessarily.

I propose Albrecht's Law, which says:

If you only pay attention to the things that go wrong, then you think Murphy's Law holds true.

DEALING WITH THE PESSIMISTS

When you are trying to launch a new venture in an organization, the first people you usually hear from are the ones in the "Department of Why It Won't Work." You need to understand this fact, take it in stride, adapt to it, and not fret about it. You don't have to hate the pessimists, but you do have to come to terms with them sooner or later.

Positive thinkers are optimistic thinkers. It is amusing sometimes to see how much they tend to irritate certain kinds of people by their very optimism. It is a peculiar fact in our world that a positive thinker is sometimes labeled a screwball. Optimists are often depicted as somewhat scatterbrained, overly amiable, and often exasperating people. Many people roll their eyes in despair when they meet someone they feel is an overly optimistic person, bubbling with new ideas. The corporate paraphrase of Rudyard

Kipling's famous poem "If" goes: "If you can keep your head when all about you are losing theirs, then you probably don't understand the situation."

Optimistic thinkers can use two strategies to deal with the pessimists. If it's feasible and practical, they can bypass these people altogether. Sometimes the most vocal critics have little or nothing to do with a current project. They can afford to criticize an idea or a strategic plan because they are not involved in the outcome. If they don't have any clout in the situation, perhaps you can afford to ignore them.

The second option is to carefully sell the idea to the pessimistic, negative thinkers of the company. The old saying "If you can't beat'em, join'em" applies here. Often the best way to convince the pessimists about the value of an idea is to explain *their* role and function in the implementation of the idea. When they see they have a definite part to play, they may change their minds and become more receptive to your plans.

DEVELOPING POSITIVE HABITS

One of the first steps you can take to improve your positive outlook is to *stop complaining!* That's it, just stop complaining about everything. It rarely helps anyway, and when it does, it's usually only coupled with positive actions geared toward creative problem solving. While negative thinkers complain about their lot, positive thinkers try to improve theirs.

Think of your friends and acquaintances. Do you like to spend time with people who complain about things all the time? Probably not. How do others perceive you? Do you have trouble getting along with other people because you gripe about things? Negative thoughts and statements not only hold you back, they weigh other people down as well. People try to avoid a complaining person because they don't like to listen to a constant stream of depressing problems or gripes. We all have problems, and most people dislike being burdened with the complaints of others. Complaints about the traffic, the weather, the local baseball team, and taxes may feel good to the negative thinker, but the positive thinker knows most of these complaints are not constructive.

Positive people within a creative organization know not to complain about the things they cannot control. Chronic complaining generates bad feelings throughout the organization. Continuous complaints about minor inequities, such as the lack of parking in the company lot or other trivialities, do little to spur creative thinking. In fact, these types of complaints often drive morale down and cause people to bicker among themselves. Chronic complaining works hand in hand with constant criticism, an obvious part of idea killing. Notice that the chronic complainers in an organization are usually also the idea killers in the crowd.

In this connection, Thomas Jefferson once remarked, "I complained about having no shoes until I met a man who had no feet." This quotation illustrates a good point. It's easy to complain about why you are not doing better than your peers, but it's hard to refute the fact that most of us go to bed well-fed and warm each night.

Margaret McGee, a San Diego-based educational specialist says, "Think about the level from which you are complaining. Did you know that nearly half of the world's population goes to bed hungry every night? This is something to keep in mind the next time you complain about the high cost of your grocery bill or restaurant check."

You can reduce plenty of complaints to infinitesimal levels when you consider your present perspective. Don't complain about your car if you have one, because there are many people that can't afford one or don't even know how to drive. Don't complain about the high cost of heating or cooling your house because many people live on the streets. Recognize the level from which you are complaining. Realize that you are reasonably healthy, successful, and happy. Appreciate what you have and be thankful for it. As Scrooge's Bob Cratchit said when he donated some of his meager wages to charity, "There are others in worse situations than me."

Another thing you can do to become more positive is to *stop worrying!* Nothing comes from worrying about the unknown. If you must, worry about what you know: the mortgage, your kid's braces, the peeling paint at your house. Too many people spend too much time worrying about what they cannot possibly control. Worry often leads to apprehension which leads to anxiety. Anxiety is very difficult to control once it takes hold of you.

Anxiety and the accompanying stress symptoms are also physically harmful to you as a creative thinker. Tests have shown that most people don't think well under the stress of an anxiety-laden situation. So-called snap decisions are not usually creatively based decisions. Anxiety and stress work to inhibit your creative ability. When you come to work preoccupied and tense, you rarely feel like thinking creatively.

What causes worry anyway? Most people worry because they are uncertain about the future. Our biggest worries relate to our careers, our love relationships, and money, though not necessarily in that order. Time spent worrying is usually wasted time. The people who spend the least amount of time worrying are those who have spent the most time planning.

As one highly skilled police officer once told me, "I never worry about what will happen when I get to a radio call. I spend my time driving safely and carefully to the scene. I plan my strategy, considering all the possibilities. When I get to the scene, I take the appropriate actions I feel are necessary. I am aware, not worried." Here, planning is the key to this officer's safety and success. This should be your strategy in your own business and personal life.

POSITIVE SELF-TALK

Positive talking is more than just optimistic talk, it's positive *self-talk* too. Positive self-talk deals with your opinion of yourself. If you think you are a creative thinker, then you will be a creative thinker. People who have healthy self-images rarely use negative terms to describe themselves.

Make it a point to rid your speech and thoughts of all forms of negative self-talk. If you're not doing it now, learn to speak positively about yourself. Revise your language to exclude this negative drain on your creativity. Think before you speak. Choose your words carefully. Concentrate on your language habits. You'll be surprised to see how far it goes to improve your self-image and the way other people perceive you as well.

Think about your friends and acquaintances who constantly talk negatively about themselves and others. These people are no fun to be with. Notice how they bring the conversation down with their negativity. Watch how you speak, and tailor your words to include a positive message each time you engage in conversation.

One of the favorite negative self-talk statements heard all the time is: "God, I'm dying for a cigarette right now." This sounds like the epitome of irony. In fact, people often use the word *die* in conversation as a negative self-expression. Examples of this misuse include, "It was so hot. I was dying out there," and "I'm dead tired."

Try to eliminate this negative vocabulary from your daily conversation. In defense of these statements people will say, "Well, you know what I really meant. I wasn't really dying." Even so, this type of negative talk is destructive to the inner model of your self-concept. When you use self-defeating words you reinforce negative feelings to yourself and others. Start talking positively about yourself.

POSITIVE VALUE JUDGMENTS

One last concept that is both important to understand and difficult to put into practice is the ability to withhold critical, uninformed evaluations of people and their ideas. This relates to opinion flexibility, and it's much easier said than done. Instead of jumping to a conclusion or making a preformed value judgment about everyone you see, withhold your feelings until you've gathered more facts.

As an example, when you are driving down the street and see a shaggy, bearded, and generally unkempt person walking along, you usually make a snap decision about the person. Most of us might have preconceived notions or prejudices about such a person's laziness, criminal record, narcotics use, and so forth. This negative evaluation is such an easy trap to fall into that we rarely notice it. It is easier to judge people on the basis of their dress and appearance than on what they have to say for themselves as individuals.

This occurs constantly in an organizational setting. People sometimes let their prejudices and opinions cloud their judgment when they listen to an idea proposal. This lack of flexibility may be because the person has had a bad experience in a previous assignment or because he or she may not like the person presenting the idea for one reason or another. Many qualified people are shut off from the manager's office because of the way they dress or appear to behave. Witness the categorizing of the highly creative but seemingly eccentric computer engineers who are often called *propeller heads* by office skeptics.

Computer people are often poorly dressed and generally unkempt in appearance. This stigma may interfere with your ability to fairly judge their creative thoughts and ideas. Even though a person appears uncivilized, he or she may actually be quite intelligent. Don't let someone's appearance or behavior deter you from listening to his or her ideas. Some of our brightest inventors have been written off as crackpots. Don't make this same mistake in your organization.

Such negative evaluation also does little to enhance your image as a creative person. If you express your negative opinions out loud, it may tend to stifle the opinions of your co-workers. While it's easy to say all of this, it's also very difficult to put into play. However, your negative evaluations of people and their ideas both does little to help your creativity and is also destructive to your own feelings of self-worth as well.

Your emotional state has a lot to do with your creativity. Remember, negative feelings stifle creative thoughts and positive feelings help stimulate your creative and innovative thoughts. Recognize that you base your positive thinking on your own frame of reference. How others perceive you as a creative person often depends on whether or not you see yourself as a positive person. Your interior feelings are greatly influenced by what you say and how you think. Why go through life filling yourself and other people up with negative thoughts, images, and feelings? Learn to see the positive side of any situation, no matter how uncertain it may appear at first. The optimist sees the opportunity for growth and benefits in all of his or her experiences. Appreciate the positive side of any situation and see how it improves your capacity for creative thought.

Here's another example of the power of optimistic, flexible thought: Two scientists were trying to develop a new type of industrial dye. After many months of work, they still did not have a usable dye, but they had come up with a new type of insect repellent. Question: Does this mean they failed? The negative thinker might say yes, but the positive thinker would see the situation as a creative victory, anyway. Keep this in mind:

Things work out for the best if you know how to make the best of the way things work out.

CHAPTER TEN

The Power of Words in Human Thought

"In Paris they simply stared at me when I spoke to them in French. I never did succeed in making those idiots understand their own language."

MARK TWAIN

There is a mysterious psychology to the use of human language. Your understanding of this unconscious language psychology can help make you more creative. It can also increase the impact you have on others. If you know how language affects the human mind, you can think more clearly, understand yourself and your world better, and get through to other people more effectively.

We know from research and the study of group dynamics that group members will naturally gravitate toward the person who is the most positively vocal and persuasive. Studies have shown that in a group situation, the most influential person is often the one who first sits quietly and observes the needs of the group and then responds by directing their energies toward his or her own ideas. This is done in such a subtle fashion that it's not even recognized by the group members. This is often because by the time the leader steps in to exert his or her influence, the group has already wasted time and sidetracked itself with infighting, overorganization, and other common group-related problems.

It is important for the group to perceive the leader as someone who has his or her own interests in mind as well as the best interests of the whole group. The move toward taking control of the direction and focus of the group's energies should not be seen as a power play but rather as a way of channeling the group efforts. How you speak, the words you choose, and your ability to communicate your ideas to other influential people are the keys to your success as a creative thinker.

Warren Bennis, the noted business professor from the University of Southern California, conducted a study about the nature of executive personalities. One of the things he noticed as he interviewed 90 well-recognized leaders was how articulate they all were in a persuasive and conceptual way. Bennis found that his effective leaders used certain conversational techniques to induce other people—in a subtle fashion—to accept their way of looking at things. They were skilled at gaining control of the frame of reference of the conversation by offering powerful metaphors and analogies in order to make their points.

After Bennis pointed out this phenomenon, I began to become highly aware of it in my conversation with various high-influence people. I refer to it as *frame-of-reference control*. By offering an organizing concept, a ringing statement, or a strong metaphor as a part of the way he or she presents an idea, the leader builds an invisible framework around the thoughts of others. They respond unconsciously to this useful frame of reference and accept it as a model for their own points of view. In providing the organizing frame, the leader puts people on a mental track of his or her choosing. This makes it easier to guide their thoughts and reactions in the direction of the conclusion the leader wants to sell. The process is usually unconscious, and the respondents tend to see the presentation of the organizing frame as a form of behavior appropriate to a leader.

Group members accept this conceptual fluency and skilled use of language as a form of potency on the leader's part. The use of metaphors, analogies, similes, and other powerful figures of speech as a part of an entire power-based vocabulary enables the leader to shape the sense and direction of the conversation. Clearly, Bennis found it was the language structures that the speaker used, as well as the ideas presented, that *earned* the acceptance of the listeners and induced them to unconsciously elect the high-influence person to a leadership role.

You can apply this concept to build your own skills as an effective communicator and leader. You can do certain things that make others perceive you as a powerful conversationalist and innovative thinker. When you become involved in a group or face-to-face discussion about some problem or project, you can make certain key statements that offer this kind of subtle influence. "Where are we?" "What's our objective?" and "How do we get there?" are all statements you can use to guide the direction of a discussion or a meeting. If offered helpfully and in a nonthreatening manner, these statements will be heard by other people as "take-charge" statements. Your use of them can show others that you have the desired capabilities and can handle the leadership role within the group.

To clarify this point in your own mind, you can begin by listening for such statements in conversations with people you perceive to be effective leaders and communicators. Think about a CEO or a high-level manager you know. Next time you are in a group problem-solving situation, watch this person's actions, reactions, and the general tone of the conversation. How does this person take charge with his or her language?

Note that this type of behavior is rarely seen as pushy by other group members because it is a positive, encouraging, and goal-oriented behavior for the good of the entire group. The leader is really performing a service for the group while helping them to see things his or her way.

Dynamic group leaders and problem solvers usually follow a pattern. In the beginning they watch the actions and dialogue of the group without much comment. At this point they are somewhat ambiguous. After watching the direction of the group and seeing which members have the strongest personalities, this person will wait for an appropriate opportunity to contribute a helping action. Often, when the level of conflict is high, the leader will step in and offer a well-placed comment or a suggestion that resolves the difficulty and helps the members refocus their attention in a more effective way. From that point the leader can use his or her newly earned influence to shape the new direction of the group.

USING METAPHORS

People who can communicate their ideas powerfully are often skilled makers and users of *metaphors*. A metaphor is a figure of speech, a phrase or idea that lets you replace an abstract thought with a concrete concept. If people have trouble following you when you describe a new idea in abstract terms, you can concretize it for them by invoking a suitable metaphor.

We use metaphors extensively in our language habits every day. The skilled use of metaphor goes beyond the completely routinized figures of speech and creates new metaphors to catch the comprehension of the listener. Businesspeople frequently use metaphorical expressions to convey an idea to someone else. "Get rid of that alligator" (an unsuccessful venture that is a financial drain on the company); "That would be like trying to turn the *Queen Mary*" (trying to change the habits of a large number of people); and "Can't you read the handwriting on the wall?" (possible news of an impending disaster).

Do you see how these metaphors can convert a seemingly abstract concept into concrete and understandable terms? The original idea is somewhat vague, diffuse, and intangible. The substitute metaphor is concrete, tangible, and something the listener can see, hear, feel, smell, or taste in his or her own mind.

USING ANALOGIES

Using analogies is another useful way to explain abstract concepts in concrete terms. An analogy shows someone that one thing is often like another, even though the two seem unrelated at first. The best time to use an analogy is when you need to explain something that your listeners have never seen before. A concise analogy can transfer their understanding of your message from the familiar to the unfamiliar.

Let's say a group of people work for a computer software publishing firm. They are having a meeting to decide on a pricing policy for their new software product. While they struggle with the problem, one of the group members decides to invoke an analogy in hopes of clarifying the problem. He tells the group that a software product is much like a book. A software program is an information product, just like a book. They are both the same relative size and shape, and they both cost about the same to manufacture. This leads to considerations of marketing the software package in ways similar to those used for books.

Every analogy has its limitations. The two things are not the same in all respects, so it is important to avoid the trap of extending the analogy beyond its range of applicability. Software programs may take many thousands of hours to create, while a book may involve a few hundred hours. The distribution process for a software program is not as widely available as a book. The channels of selling and marketing the product are different. Thus the pricing strategy has to be different as well.

Note that the limitations of the analogy may actually help the thinking process. By asking "How is a software package *different* from a book?" the planners clarify their understanding of the big picture. Similarities help to focus attention and simplify discussion. Differences help to bring out the unique factors that deserve attention as well.

USING SIMILES

Similes are figures of speech that offer us another way to compare people, places, or objects. We can immediately recognize the language in a simile and relate it to something else. "She's as cold as ice" conveys a certain message to the listener. From this the listener understands the woman in question may be rigid, aloof, or unfriendly. "He's as subtle as a herd of elephants" conveys, by the use of irony, that the man is socially forward and lacks a sense of grace or poise in dealing with people. "Dead as a doornail" conjures up its own visual message. Doornails are unmoving, inanimate objects. The simile suggests lifelessness, immobility, and a nonhuman quality. "Light as a feather" conveys something that is soft, delicate, and easy to handle.

We use these terms routinely and even unconsciously in everyday conversation because in most cases, the listener immediately understands what we mean without further explanation. They add color and energy to our conversations. Taken literally, metaphors and similes often make no sense at all. People from foreign countries often have difficulty interpreting our frequent use of metaphors and similes. It's important to keep this concept in mind as you deal with someone whose command of English may not be the same as yours. Metaphors, similes, and analogies are only useful communication devices if both parties understand the idea in the first place.

Semanticist S. I. Hayakawa referred to metaphors as the *ornaments of speech*. You can improve your conversations by including some of these ornaments in the right places. Business exchanges don't always have to be dry and direct. See how you can add color to your conversations.

Men tend to make more frequent use of metaphors and analogies than women. Partly because of social conditioning, men tend to use figures of speech that relate to sports, battle, combat, and war. Some examples of this include "Don't drop the ball this time," "Go out there and fight fire with fire," "He shot down my idea," and "Let's hit 'em while their flanks are exposed." This language is frequently heard in sales and marketing meetings whose main purpose is often only to "whip up the troops."

As a general rule, women in business don't usually exhibit this kind of conversational behavior. Women in management often speak in terms of people and feelings rather than power-based actions or reactions. It is for this reason that many male managers may feel that female managers lack power because their entire vocabularies are often vastly different. This inability or lack of desire to use male-oriented, so-called power words and phrases may actually hinder a woman's ability to gain influence in a male-dominated business environment. This is not to say that women should try to imitate men and give up their femininity in order to succeed in business.

The key to mastering this type of power-based vocabulary is *subtlety*. Remember that in most cases where someone used concrete descriptions and power words to successfully take control of a group or meeting, it was done in a subtle fashion. Powerful, creative leaders can steer others toward their point of view without posturing, browbeating, or threatening them.

DEVELOPING YOUR METAPHORICAL SKILLS

Take a sheet of paper and a pen and see how many different figures of speech you can think of to express the word *crazy*. When you finish, see how many words or phrases you can come up with to describe a mental hospital. Be creative, humorous, and innovative. Come back to the book when you've finished both lists.

Figures of speech for *crazy*
> Nobody home upstairs.
> All of his biscuits aren't baked.

Not playing with a full deck.
Off in his upper story.
Doesn't have both oars in the water.
Not wrapped too tight.
His brains are scrambled.
He's got a screw loose.
Not all there.
Lives in his own little world.
Hears a different drummer.

Figures of speech for mental hospital
The nut house.
The laughing academy.
The hotel silly.
The funny farm.
The hotel for the disenchanted.
The loony bin.
The headshrinker's house.
The psycho ward.
The wacko ward.
The crazy house.
The cuckoo house.

How many of your examples agreed with the above list? I'll bet you could think of at least that many and more. The importance of this practice exercise is to show you there are many different ways of expressing an idea to someone. You could show these two lists to almost anyone and they would instantly understand which frame of mind (*crazy*), and which place (*a mental hospital*) you were talking about. That is the real value of metaphors; they are tools for communication.

IMPROVING YOUR CONCEPTUAL VOCABULARY

It's no accident that people who are highly influential in business situations and leadership roles tend to be more articulate than others. Effective leaders are almost all distinguished by a fine-tuned command of the written and spoken word. Successful business leaders usually have vastly larger and more flexible vocabularies than most other people. They can use a well-turned phrase to express an entire concept. They can speak simply and powerfully when one situation calls for it, and eloquently when another situation calls for it.

Think about your own language habits. Do you feel you have a good grasp of the written and spoken word? Many business-people can express themselves quite eloquently in person, but can't write a clear memo. Other people can write beautiful reports, yet can't stand in front of a group and give a straightforward presentation. The best business leaders can do both quite well.

If you have difficulty getting other people to take you and your ideas seriously, stop and evaluate your use of language. There's a good possibility that you may lack the proper word skills to be convincing in interpersonal situations. Concentrate on improving your language skills and habits over the next few months.

In general, people have a much larger recognition vocabulary than speaking vocabulary. This means that they recognize far more words than they ever use in normal conversation. One of the keys to improving your conceptual fluency—and the way that other people perceive you as an effective leader and speaker—is to incorporate more *conceptual fluency* terms into your vocabulary. A conceptual fluency term is one that helps you to explain a concept by crystallizing it so other people will understand it as well.

The leader in the study and use of conceptual fluency words is the British author and creativity guru Edward de Bono. His book, *Wordpower: An Illustrated Dictionary of Vital Words* is a classic of its kind.[1] De Bono makes an interesting point about how others perceive you by the use of your words. "The difference," he writes, "between an educated and an uneducated person is not usually a matter of intelligence or even knowledge. It is simply that the educated person has a bigger stock of concepts with which to express himself."[2]

De Bono chooses the word *trade-off"* as an example of a useful conceptual term. A trade-off is a choice between two different alternatives, where you can choose one or the other, but not both. Each option has certain appealing features which the other lacks. You have to be willing to trade some features for other features in order to settle on a solution.

For example, you are offered a sales position at a relatively large corporation. The sales manager tells you to decide how you want to be paid. You can accept a big salary and a small commission, or take a small salary and a large commission. Both sides of this trade-off require some thought. You must decide what is right for you and what offers you the most benefits. The trade-off is security versus the potential for a large income.

According to de Bono's theory, the person who knows *and uses* the term *trade-off* is "smarter" in a way than the person who doesn't. Without knowing and using the term, or some similarly useful term, the person trying to express his or her ideas must grope around inefficiently. He or she lacks the conceptual facility simply by lacking the term.

Conceptual fluency terms put handles on your ideas and thoughts. They help you grasp certain concepts by crystallizing them in your own mind and in the minds of others. Business leaders have extensive and powerful conceptual vocabularies. They are rarely at a loss for words. Try to incorporate conceptual fluency words into your own language habits. Study the list of de Bono's examples for some help:

ad hoc.   An ad hoc approach is one that is not permanent, but is devised to solve the problem at hand. Using a paper clip as a temporary button is an ad hoc solution.

asset.   A tangible or intangible possession that has value to you. It doesn't always have to be "liquid" like cash; good health is an asset too.

cash cow.   A profitable product that can be "milked" for money, without having to be tended on a continual basis. A best-selling book which makes the author a large amount of money from its royalties is a cash cow.

Catch-22.   From the Joseph Heller novel of the same name. A no-win situation. You can't get a job unless you have experience and you can't get experience without a job; that's Catch-22.

crystallize.   Crystallizing something, in the metaphorical sense, usually clarifies it and reduces any attached ambiguity. Your plan may help you to crystallize your personal desires into a clear set of goals.

downside risk.   Weighing the possible negative outcome of a prospective venture. Comparing what you might gain versus what is at stake to lose. A term taken from stock market analysis.

eclectic.   Making a choice based on a combination of the best of the different options around you. If your choices in furniture are eclectic, you may mix various styles into a combination you like.

extrapolate.   To estimate a future situation by assuming that a current trend will continue to hold true for some period of time. Business forecasts are often made using the extrapolation of past information. If sales are growing at 10 percent per year, you might extrapolate your current sales volume for the next few years by assuming the 10 percent growth will continue. Remember, of course, that it may not. You must be highly conscious of your extrapolations.

feedback.   Information that tells you what effect your action has produced. Customer feedback can tell you how good a job you are doing in delivering your service. Employee feedback can tell you how well you are managing the organization. "Closing the (feedback) loop" means getting feedback information and changing your actions based on what the feedback tells you.

filter.   A device that removes some things and lets other things pass through. Psychologists say we all see the world through the filter of our own individual experience. Information sometimes gets filtered as it passes along the channels in an organization.

hedge.   To limit the amount of risk involved in a course of action by having a backup plan or an alternative way to accomplish the same thing.

hierarchy.   An organized structure involving defined levels and subdivisions. Often related to the formal and informal networks in an organization. Psychologist Abraham Maslow said we human beings have a hierarchy of needs, that is, a structured set of needs that have different levels of priority for us.

inertia.   The inertia of any object, person, or organization is its reluctance to move. A manager displays a lot of inertia when he or she fails to take action on an important matter.

metasystem.   The system which is outside or beyond the current system you are thinking about. Farmers grow their own food and the food of a nation.

payoff.   Often referred to as the *reason for all actions*. Businesspeople wait for it as the fruit of all their efforts. It can come in the form of money, goodwill, or future gains. To understand a person's behavior, ask yourself, "What payoff is he or she getting for acting that way?"

polarize.   Creating two opposite ends and pushing all the views toward one end or the other. A certain problem or issue might polarize opinion sharply in the organization. Two groups might be strongly polarized on a certain point.

quantum jump.   A significant increase in some measurement. A quantum jump in the number of orders placed for a product is usually something to celebrate.

rationale.   A logical explanation for doing something. When you explain your rationale for launching a project, someone else can understand the logical reasoning process you went through to make your decision.

strategy versus tactics. Strategy is a general course of action while tactics are the specific means for carrying out the course of action. Generals employ strategies in battle; soldiers use tactics to carry the strategies out. Your career strategy might involve changing to a job in a different industry. Your current tactic might be to wait for your next raise so you can negotiate a higher raise with a new company.

universe. The complete set of choices to be considered. The universe of customers for flea collars includes dog owners. Does it include cat owners?

Many of de Bono's fluency terms (he proposes over 250 of them in his book) are familiar to many people. However, there is a big difference between knowing about them and using them deliberately in your conversation. If you never use them, you will be stuck at the concrete level. You will have difficulty conveying your ideas forcefully as well as difficulty in capturing the minds of the people you want to influence.

The real beauty of these and many other conceptual fluency terms is that they add a certain crispness to your speech. They are power-based words which you can use for your own benefit. These are not fashionable "buzzwords" to be dropped at cocktail parties to prove your literacy, but rather a more powerful way to communicate your ideas to others. The point is, the more conscious you are of the psychology of language, the more clearly you can think and the more impact you have on the thoughts of others.

NOTES

[1] Edward de Bono, *Wordpower* (New York: Harper & Row, 1977).
[2] Ibid., p. 2.

CHAPTER ELEVEN

Dealing with Idea Killers

"Man is so constituted as to see what is wrong with a new thing, not what is right. To verify this, you have but to submit a new idea to a committee. They will obliterate 90 percent of rightness for the sake of 10 percent of wrongness.
The possibilities a new idea opens up are not visualized, because not one person in a thousand has imagination."

CHARLES F. KETTERING

What happens when you have a great idea and you want to tell someone about it? During the middle of your explanation, the person listening to your idea suddenly comes up with a dozen reasons why it won't work. You've just met the idea killer. This is the person who habitually reacts to the new and the novel with a negative, critical, fault-finding attitude.

Idea killers are not inherently evil people. They are normal, ordinary people. That's the trouble. Idea killing is a normal, ordinary form of behavior. Lots of people do it. Most don't do it maliciously, and many do it unconsciously. They simply don't have the open-mindedness, flexibility, and creative orientation to support the ideation processes of others. The simple fact is:

There are more idea killers than there are idea thinker-uppers.

Note that the idea killer is not a separate subspecies of the human population. Idea killing is more of a *role* that people play when their egos get involved in a new situation. Very few people are idea killers all the time. Unfortunately, however, some people make such a habit of it that they truly deserve the label of idea killer.

People shoot down another's ideas for one or both of two reasons. First, they enjoy playing the role of judge of other people.

It makes them feel powerful in a small way, even if only for a few seconds, to assume the role of approver or disapprover of the accomplishments of others.

A person who enthusiastically shares an idea, or a personal plan, or a new scheme with another person unconsciously confers on that person a degree of social authority as the listener. Since most people feel rather powerless in their lives much of the time, most of them will jump at a chance to get "one up." Rather than listen supportively, idea killers immediately get distracted by the opportunity to put the other person in his or her place. The psychological agenda of the teller is to get support and appreciation for his or her creation. But the agenda of the hearer may be to feel potent by playing a parental role and disapproving of the teller's idea.

The second reason for idea killing is simple unconscious jealousy. People who don't see themselves as very smart or creative feel an internal twinge of inferiority whenever they hear someone discussing big ideas. The idea killing put-down is a way of saying, "See? You aren't so smart. You thought your idea was such a big deal, but I just proved it won't work." This protects the idea killer from his feeling of apprehension that other people will see him or her as inferior and the idea person as capable and worthwhile.

MEET "IKE"

If you are going to have good ideas and sell them to others in the organization, you must be able to deal effectively with the chronic idea killers you are bound to encounter. You need to understand how the habitual idea killer thinks, feels, and behaves, and how to combat his or her toxic conversational habits.

Let's create a profile that is a stereotype of the quintessential idea killer. Meet "Ike" whose initials stand for "I Kill Everything." Don't let the metaphorical choice of a male name for this character role imply that women don't act this way as often as men. There is a little bit of Ike in all of us.

Ike is not really a bad guy, in general. Around the office watercooler he can be kind of friendly. However, Ike's personality changes when he goes to a staff meeting or becomes a member of a committee project. It's during these times that Ike snap-reacts as an idea killer.

Ike is unenlightened about communicating with others, which often means allowing the free trade of ideas. Look at some of the characteristics that make up Ike's personality. Compare these attitudes and habits of thought to those discussed in the chapter on mental flexibility.

One of the biggest problems that plagues Ike is his low sense of mental flexibility. Ike rarely exhibits much tolerance for ambiguity. He hates it when a situation is unresolved in any way. He likes to make definite decisions, even if these decisions may be wrong.

He hates uncertainty, and unfamiliar situations make him nervous. He would rather not deal with a complex question that emphasizes values and opinions instead of hard-and-fast facts. Long-term studies and advanced planning are a waste of time for Ike. He likes the immediate decision. He doesn't care if all of the facts are not clear or apparent. He likes to "shoot from the hip" and decide on a plan right away. The faster Ike can push the group into accepting his opinion, the sooner he can get out of the meeting. Remember that many idea killers feel uncomfortable in a group setting. Ike likes to clobber all the "goofy creative-types" in the group right away. This way, he can get his point across as soon as possible.

Ike's opinions are not very flexible either. He can't seem to hold his opinions in check until all the facts are in. He doesn't appreciate the points of view of others, and he likes to voice his own opinion, often in an aggressive manner. He often resorts to standard idea-stopping statements in expressing his opinions. Ike's own interests are usually what matter most to him. How a decision will affect his department and his office are of primary importance. Ike typically lacks team player skills. What's good for the entire organization will not receive Ike's support unless it's clearly good for him first.

Ike also typically lacks a sense of semantic flexibility. He habitually uses dogmatic, rigid statements to express himself. This lack of flexibility in his language also translates itself into a characteristic lack of flexibility in Ike's thinking skills. Ike finds safety in stock answers. When an idea doesn't meet with his approval, he just goes down his idea-stopping list until he finds a reason.

Ike has little if any positive orientation. He often wallows in negative thoughts and statements. Rather than looking at life as a series of positive events, Ike habitually complains about whatever raw deal he thinks he's getting. He loves to quote Murphy's Law and lacks a sense of humor. Instead of laughing at life's little absurdities, Ike prefers to make jokes at other people's expense. He likes to use biting humor and laughs at things that make other people appear foolish. His conversation is often laced with sarcasm and left-handed compliments. He is also a master of the "I told you it wouldn't work" lines. His hindsight is always 20–20, and he can spot the weaknesses in any plan before it even gets off the ground.

Ike has no real sense of an investigative orientation. He doesn't like to do any type of research, and he does not make a habit of seeking out new or relevant information. He dislikes it when other people try to back up their ideas with elaborate research projects and seemingly irrelevant evidence. He cannot back up his own ideas with solid research because he does not know how to use the resources available to him. Consequently, Ike frequently goes off "half-cocked."

Finally, we know that Ike has a crap detector. However, his resistance to enculturation—the ability to look at his own surroundings with an open mind—lacks continuity. He tends to be cynical and suspicious, looking for evidence that just about everybody is on the make. He often lumps things together into simple categories as a way of coping with people and their new and often threatening (to him) ideas. This tendency to categorize things can foul up his view of a new venture before it begins. He tends to be jaded, cynical, and skeptical just when he needs to be open and innocent in his perceptions.

These are just some of the components of mental flexibility that Ike lacks. Among his other patterns, he is overly ego-involved with his opinions and his need to be right. He likes to get into a battle of wills with other people to prove he is right as he tries to demolish their positions. He frequently personalizes these arguments, allowing his own feelings and emotions to get in the way of the situation at hand. This is when Ike is at his most dangerous—when his ego is totally immersed in the dispute.

Ike is handicapped by a weak self-concept. He compensates for this by bullying his way into conversations and meetings, voicing his opinions and interpretations as the benchmarks for other people to follow. He resents the ramblings of so-called idea people, who are always bombarding him with their off-the-wall ideas. He resents the way these people like to drag out a meeting by discussing new options instead of just settling on the first relatively feasible plan.

Since Ike hasn't learned the creative process, he rarely has a new or unique idea himself. He cuts himself off from learning opportunities that might help him become a more creative thinker. He unconsciously avoids opportunities to nurture his own creativity because it might take the fun out of his role as the corporate idea killer.

IDEA STOPPERS

Ike's typical weapon is a verbal "bullet," that is, something he or she says to shoot down your idea. If you think about the various encounters you've had with idea killers in your organization, you'll probably recall certain killer statements they tend to use regularly.

I call these statements *idea stoppers*. As you go down the following list, see how many of the statements sound familiar in your own organizational setting. Who in your company uses these same statements on a daily basis to kill new ideas? Do these statements fly about in your committee meetings or group projects? Are you guilty of any of them?

Idea stoppers
1. Naah.
2. Can't (said with a shake of the head and an air of finality).
3. That's the dumbest thing I've ever heard.
4. Yeah, but if you did that . . . (poses extreme or unlikely disaster case).
5. Our business is different; you can't do that here.
6. Our system isn't set up to do it that way.
7. We already tried that—years ago.
8. Look, you can't teach an old dog new tricks.
9. That's not our bailiwick.
10. Let's stick with what we know.
11. We've done all right so far; why do we need that?
12. I don't see anything wrong with the way we're doing it now.
13. That doesn't sound too practical.

14. We've never done anything like that before.
15. You're talking about changing the whole way we do things!
16. Let's not go off on a tangent.
17. Let's not get into another hare-brained scheme.
18. Let's get back to reality (business, the topic at hand, etc.).
19. We've got a deadline to meet, we don't have time to fool around with crazy ideas.
20. It's too expensive to do it that way.
21. It's not in the budget.
22. Top management (the union, the customer, etc.) will never go for that.
23. Let's take that up some other time.
24. We'll look like a bunch of nitwits doing something like that.
25. Are you kidding?
26. Who let him (or her) in here?
27. Where do you get these weird ideas?

These are just a few examples of the idea-stopping statements that idea killers frequently use in their conversation. You've probably heard many of these and more in your dealings with the idea killers in your organization. The purpose of each statement is to kill an idea that might threaten the established order, make the idea killer look smart, and make the idea haver look dumb.

BE AN IDEA HELPER

Contrast Ike the idea killer and yourself as a creative, innovative thinker. Look at some of your habits—the ones that make you an *idea helper* rather than an idea killer. What is an idea helper? It is someone who realizes that ideas, in and of themselves, are fundamentally valuable; they represent intellectual wealth. In contrast to the idea killer, the idea helper actually helps other people have and express new ideas. By reacting divergently, imaginatively, and supportively to new ideas, this person makes other people more comfortable and encourages them to think creatively.

Instead of converging on a new idea too soon, attacking the idea haver, or demanding proof that the idea is a good one, the idea helper simply assists the idea haver in developing his or her idea and clarifying it. By being ego-neutral, the idea helper plays a useful, supportive role. He or she doesn't try to seize ownership of the idea, bend it out of shape, or supersede it with a new interpretation. The trick is simply to be supportive of the idea haver's subtle, flowing thought process, and to help it bear fruit.

Idea helpers are open-minded. They *like* to hear new ideas, new points of view, and refreshing interpretations of problems and issues. They are skilled at suspending judgment and approaching a new concept innocently and without fixed opinions. They are good listeners, and they try not to cut someone off, especially when that person is in the midst of explaining a new idea. The idea helper is usually good at *active listening*, the habit of paraphrasing the speaker and asking open-ended questions that help the person express his or her views more comfortably. Idea helpers think, act, and speak as if a newly proposed idea is "innocent until proven guilty." This is not to say that they feel obligated to fully agree with everybody's new idea, or that they may not later turn it down in favor of other approaches. They just proceed with suspended judgment, knowing that making value judgments about the idea is always an available option.

In group activities and meetings, the idea helper advocates a contest of ideas, rather than a contest of personalities. He or she is not interested in doing battle over issues, but in discerning successful solutions.

IDEA SELLING

It is not enough to be creative and to have good ideas. It is not enough to be supportive of other people and help them have good ideas. You also need to be able to prevent the idea killer from doing his or her dirty work. You need specific tactics for getting around the negativism, cynicism, and criticism that come with idea-killing reactions.

The best antidote for idea killing is to prevent it, not to struggle against it. You need to know how to stop the idea killer in his tracks. You can do this very effectively many times by using a subtle verbal technique that cuts the idea-killing reaction off at the pass, so to speak. It is possible to trick most people into reacting open-mindedly in many situations.

Part of idea killing is an overly convergent mental reaction to what has just been said. The verbal trick you can use is to say something that causes the listener to slip into a divergent frame of mind, at least for a moment or two. *Idea sellers* are special statements that help you do this.

Instead of just blurting out your bright new idea and having convergent-thinking people jump all over it, you need to reach inside their minds, so to speak, and prepare their thinking for the idea. By preceding your idea-statement with one of the following idea sellers, you can often flip a mental switch in the listener's brain, and cause him or her to react more divergently and open-mindedly.

Idea sellers
1. May I ask a question?
2. Before we make a final decision, let's review the options.
3. I suggest we not eliminate any options at this point.
4. Are we ready to close the question? Have we considered all of the key factors?
5. Can we stop for a second and look at the way that we are approaching this problem?
6. I'd like to back up a step and clear up a point I don't understand.
7. I hope we don't have a case of "groupthink" here.
8. I've been hearing about X lately. Do you have any information on it?
9. I don't know much about that. How about you?
10. Were you aware that . . .?
11. There are a couple of new factors you might not know about.
12. Maybe we should reconsider (reopen, reanalyze, redecide) that point.
13. Maybe you'd like to reconsider your approach on that, since
    . . . .
14. I've changed my mind on that; I found out that . . . .
15. This idea might sound a little strange, so let me explain the whole thing first.
16. You probably don't want to make a decision on this right now, but . . . .
17. I have an idea I'd like to share with you sometime.
18. I'd like to get your help on an idea I'm trying to work out.
19. Let me ask you for some ideas on . . . .
20. Here's a half-baked idea; I don't know how it will strike you but I'll share it.

21. Here's a partly baked idea; maybe you can add something to it.
22. We'd probably better start thinking about how we're going to . . . .
23. What options do you see at this point?
24. How many ways can we . . .? What are some of the ways we can . . .?
25. Have you considered doing it by the X method?

Note the use of qualifiers and semantically flexible structures in many of these idea sellers. In this context, the use of softer, nondogmatic statements minimizes the ego involvement on your part and reduces the temptation to react parentally on the part of the listener. Using the words, "May I . . .," or "You probably . . .," seems rather low-key, but it is crucial to the health of the idea that you do not ram your point of view down your listener's throat.

Notice that in many of the idea-selling statements, the speaker admits he or she does not have all of the available information and is actively seeking help. This help may come in the form of opinions, new information, or an answer based on past experiences or expertise.

Think of your own reactions when people came to you with a budding idea of their own. Weren't you far more receptive to their points when they asked you for help or advice? Most of us welcome the challenge of a new idea to which we can add strength and depth. When others seek your advice or your particular area of expertise, you feel more like making a contribution. This is where the idea killers in the organization miss the boat. They offer such dogmatic, negative reactions that few people want to risk coming to them with a new or untried idea.

The idea-selling statements listed above are also sometimes called *prep statements*, as in statements that prepare the listener for your idea. Many of the statements ask the listener to generate his or her own options, based on the idea the speaker wishes to discuss. Helping your listener see that there may be other options to the problem at hand is one of the keys to selling your idea to that person.

Remember that prevention is the best strategy in dealing with the idea-killing reaction. Keep in mind that

The best way to sell an idea is to help people buy it.

THE IDEA KILLER WITHIN YOU?

Up to this point, I have discussed the traits of the idea killer, describing him or her as an obstacle you must sometimes deal with in the creative corporation. I have profiled this person in terms of rigidity, aggressive behavior, and inability to accept or generate creative ideas on his or her own. I hope I have not described any of your own traits.

If you feel you have some of these toxic habits, you can bet other people in your organization can recognize them in you, too. One of the worst possible reputations to have in any creative organization is that of an idea killer. This pegs you as an inflexible, negative thinker who destroys the ideas and tries to dominate the thoughts of others. People will not come to you with their own creative ideas, especially if you are in a supervisory role, because they find this negative input too hard to take.

If you suspect you may be a closet idea killer, now is the time to re-evaluate your interpersonal relations with your co-workers. Ask them for honest feedback. Find out how they see you. Work on becoming an idea helper. Not only can you make a worthwhile contribution to the organization through your own creative ideas and solutions but you can also empower others to do the same.

CHAPTER TWELVE

Big-Picture Thinking: The Helicopter View

"Heavier than air flying machines are impossible."

LORD KELVIN, 1895
President, Royal Society

"Everything that can be invented has been invented."

CHARLES H. DUELL, 1899
Head, U.S. Patent Office

"Sensible and responsible women do not want to vote."

GROVER CLEVELAND, 1905

"Who the hell wants to hear actors talk?"

HARRY M. WARNER, 1927
Warner Bros. Pictures

Two hens were strolling around the barnyard. Suddenly one hen stopped, looked off pensively into the distance, and remarked to the other, "Say—with all the eggs we've been laying, doesn't it seem like there should be a lot more of us around here?" That's big-picture thinking.

One of the hallmarks of the effective thinker is a well-developed conceptual skill—the ability to see the forest as well as the trees or, if you like, the barnyard as well as the chickens. In this chapter we explore the importance of conceptual thinking in helping you create valuable ideas and sell those ideas to others.

Conceptual thinking is one of those important human abilities that is virtually ignored in formal schooling. The assumption seems to be that people learn to think properly as a normal consequence of growing up and dealing with life's problems. However, it is abundantly clear that many adults—perhaps most—have developed very limited competence in conceptual thought. Most people seem to be focused more or less permanently at the concrete level of direct experience, with little facility for big-picture thinking.

The conceptual thinkers in an organization are usually the ones who establish the direction which others accept and follow. They are the "brains" of the organization. People who are not skilled at conceptual thinking may be good soldiers but they are rarely good generals. They are handicapped by their dependence on others for the broad thinking processes that are needed to solve the major problems of the organization.

Let's explore this faculty of conceptual thinking. Let's turn it over and look at it from many angles. By thinking about this type of thinking, we can figure out what the real skills are and how to develop them on a personal basis.

There are many labels for conceptual thinking. Some people call it big-picture thinking. Some call it global thinking. Psychologists call it abstract thinking. One of my favorite metaphors for it is *helicopter thinking*. This term implies the ability to rise above the "landscape" of everyday thought and see all the major factors involved at one glance. Big-picture thinking usually involves a measure of *relational thinking*, which is the process of connecting various facts and ideas and finding meaning in the combinations.

Let's start with the notion of *abstract thinking*. What is it? How does it work? And why is it important? Not only are many people not very comfortable with abstract thinking, many of them cannot even define it clearly. When you mention the term *abstract thinking*, many people draw a blank. They are not very familiar with the term, the process, or the notion itself. That is the main reason they can't do it very well.

Let's define it. Abstract thinking is the process of handling ideas that are abstract, that is, ideas that you cannot represent in concrete form. An idea is abstract when you can experience it only in your mind or your imagination. An idea is concrete when you can see, hear, feel, smell, or taste the object being discussed.

A pencil, a potato, a couch, and a paper clip are concrete objects. You are able to see these things and, with the probable exception of the couch, hold them in your hands. When you are thinking about them or talking about them as specific objects, you are thinking concretely. Concrete ideas usually deal with your senses.

What are some examples of abstract ideas? Democracy, free enterprise, fair play, commerce, citizenship, and equality are all abstract concepts. Democracy, for example, is not something you can hold in your hand. This is the nature of abstract thought: it is untouchable and has an illusory quality about it. This book you are holding is a concrete object. The words printed in it cause your mind to reflect on abstract ideas.

Actually, there is a whole range of variations between the concrete and the abstract levels. We can think of a specific concept as somewhere on a scale of abstraction, ranging from the very concrete to the very abstract. You can classify most ideas in concrete or abstract terms by thinking of a sliding scale of abstraction.

You could call the small, graphite-filled, wooden cylinder on your desk a "pencil." Or, farther up the scale, you could refer to it as a "writing implement." In another abstract sense, you could also call it a "communication device." At this point, your concept of the pencil is no longer concrete; it is now an abstraction.

Successful business thinkers are comfortable with such abstract ideas and terms as objective, strategy, plan, resources, and organization. They are intellectually aggressive enough to think on a conceptual level.

One of the important keys to thinking successfully in business is the ability to move up and down the scale of abstraction and to think and communicate at *all* levels. If you are skilled at *abstracting,* you can shift the abstraction level of your thoughts and your conversation to fit the needs of the situation. You can be comfortable when people are discussing the nitty-gritty details of a problem as well as when they are dealing with the broadest philosophical concepts.

If you are fluent and comfortable with big-picture thinking, you can talk knowledgeably with executives about the overall direction and strategy of the company. If you are comfortable with details, facts, and figures, you can talk in specific terms with working people who are focused on direct experiences and concrete results. You won't need to depend on others to interpret the situation, figure things out, decide what strategies to consider. You can be the one who takes charge intellectually and provides the conceptual leadership.

GLOBAL THINKING

Effective thinkers are usually *global* thinkers as well. They have a certain breadth of knowledge, awareness, and vision that enables them to think on a grand scale as well as on an abstract level. Let's look at global thinking.

When you look at a globe of the earth, you are looking at an abstract representation of the world as a whole. Taken literally then, global thought is whole-worldly thought. It is abstract and broad based, and it entertains a wide range of considerations. As contrasted to thinking about some one specific factor, global thought involves thinking conceptually about a variety of factors. Global thought is an expansive, far-reaching type of thinking.

Your particular job, for instance, is a relatively specific, concrete factor. However, when you look at it in terms of your department or the overall organization you work for, you are thinking more globally. When you consider the entire industry that you work in, you are thinking on an even broader global level. Your job becomes a part of the entire global picture.

Global thinking is the basis for strategic thinking. Most of our history's great statesmen and intellects were also global thinkers. Jefferson, Lincoln, Churchill, and Franklin Roosevelt were global thinkers; indeed, in a literal sense their ideas and philosophies had an impact on the entire world. Their wide-ranging creativity led to the development of certain influential political, social, and humanistic ideals.

FAMOUS GLOBAL THINKERS

Who are some of the well-known figures in our history that were global thinkers? Which of these people were willing and able to conceive of the big picture? Leonardo da Vinci, Winston Churchill, Albert Einstein, and Jonas Salk come immediately to mind as global, high-level thinkers.

Leonardo da Vinci was a global thinker, especially on a technological level. His inventions and drawings were forerunners in such areas as human flight, weaponry, construction, engineering, and the study of human anatomy. His abstract viewpoint on the world allowed him to create new designs which led to modern day tools and ideas that we take for granted. His attention to detail in his drawings and paintings, together with his acute sense of conceptual design and abstract theory, made him an intellect almost without equal in his time.

Churchill's view of the world at war and his firm grasp of the politics of the European conflict made him the undisputed leader of the Allied resistance to the German onslaught. He maintained a clear, unwavering commitment to blocking the German advance and eventually destroying the insane Third Reich. It was the tremendous force of his intellect as much as the determination and strength of his personal character that made him a larger-than-life figure in the eyes of Britons and Europeans.

Albert Einstein demonstrated, through the formulations involved in his theory of relativity, an uncanny breadth of vision and conceptual grace. In working out the theory, he called into question some of the most basic assumptions of physics. Only a mind of immense conceptual dimensions could have advanced such a fundamentally new framework for the study of space and time. His work raised some difficult questions about the uses and misuses of the atom in our lives. Einstein is less remembered today for his radical concepts of pacifism, social justice, and the prevention of war, but his contributions in those areas are just as impressive conceptually as his contributions to theoretical physics.

Jonas Salk's development of the polio vaccine helped to save countless lives. He knew that his work would affect the entire world. He chose to pursue a difficult path—disease research—because he understood the significance of the undertaking for the rest of humanity.

Other global thinkers include the brilliant and eloquent statesman Thomas Jefferson, whose intellectual leadership was central to the decision of the colonial representatives to declare U.S. independence from Britain. He saw "government for the people" as exactly that: a democracy, with each person having a say in the matters that pertained to the growth and development of the community. He maintained, "That government is best which governs least." Jefferson was such a powerful conceptual thinker and a keen intellect that President John Kennedy is said to have remarked during an assemblage of leading political figures in the White House, "This may be the greatest assemblage of intellects ever to grace the White House, with the possible exception of the time when Thomas Jefferson dined alone."

HOW TO IMPROVE YOUR BIG-PICTURE SKILLS

If you don't feel as comfortable with big-picture thinking as you'd like, it may be simply because you lack confidence in your thinking processes. It is very probable that you already have the mental horsepower, that is, the basic intelligence, necessary to be a global, conceptual thinker. You may not have developed the necessary habits of thought. There are two things you can do to begin strengthening your conceptual skills.

First, make yourself much more aware of abstract ideas. Pay closer attention to the role of abstract, conceptual, and philosophical ideas in your life. And second, simply go around imitating conceptual thinkers—and talkers—whom you admire and respect. Speak their language and you will begin to think their kinds of thoughts.

You can start with a simple exercise to increase your awareness and your sense of comfort with abstract thought. Take an ordinary daily newspaper editorial, or perhaps one from your favorite magazine. Scan the article and use your pen or a felt-tipped highlight marker to underline each highly abstract word or phrase you find. Pinpoint the key abstractions in the article and see how the author uses them to frame his or her ideas.

Dwell on the various abstract terms and phrases and make them your own. Say to yourself, "I could have said it that way. I could have chosen that particular expression or figure of speech." Imagine that you yourself had written the article, using exactly the same terms. Think through each of the sentences that contains an abstract term. Make sure you understand it. Make sure you grasp the meaning and the effect of the abstract terms involved.

Read a few of the key sentences and paragraphs aloud to hear your own voice speaking these abstract terms. Make up your mind that you will find an occasion in the near future to use some of these key abstractions in conversation. Visualize yourself and hear yourself talking this way as a normal mode of conversation.

Watch also for the author's use of metaphors. As we discovered in Chapter 10, metaphors help to convert abstract concepts into concrete, understandable form. They help you express ideas fluently as you mix abstract and concrete concepts together for maximum effect in conversation.

The example I chose from my local paper deals with taxes as they pertain to the rich and the poor. The author uses such figures of speech as "harnessing the dollar," "soaking the poor," and "dealing the rich a winning hand." His use of abstract terms and concepts includes the "national coffers," the "public good," and "social approval."

Editorials provide good examples of conceptual thought because they usually deal with topics of broad interest. As you read each of your chosen samples, pay close attention to the writer's conceptual vocabulary. The skillful use of abstract concepts to build an argument implies that the writer is a conceptual thinker. By conceptual writing, I don't necessarily mean using a large vocabulary, although that is a part of it. But the fluent use of certain abstract terminology identifies the writer as someone possessed of a certain clarity of thought.

As you become more conscious of conceptual terminology in the things you read and hear other people say, make a special effort to incorporate these kinds of terms in your everyday business vocabulary. This conscious usage of abstract terminology is a critical point. Your recognition vocabulary may be very large, and you may know the meanings of many abstract words. But if you don't use them in your conversation, you probably are not using them in your thinking processes. If you continue to confine yourself to the concrete level of verbal discourse, you will confine your thoughts to that level as well. Training yourself to talk conceptually leads you to think conceptually.

Think of it as going around impersonating a conceptual thinker. Talk the way conceptual thinkers talk and you will think the way they think. I sometimes call it talking "Ph.D. talk." It is an educated, erudite, precise, and effective form of conversation. You don't have to take it to extremes, of course, but if you haven't been in the habit of using conceptual terminology there isn't much danger of overdoing it. The more you practice it, the more natural it will become.

MEET THE MIND MAP

There is a simple pen-and-paper technique that can help you develop your conceptual-relational thinking skills and, at the same time, enable you to work out more effective solutions to the problems you attack. It's called *mind-mapping*, and here is how it works.

Let's say your boss asks you to write a brief report to distribute at the next staff meeting. The topic is "How to Improve Our Sales Volume."

To begin, get yourself a pen and a generous-sized writing pad. Find a comfortable, undisturbed place to work, where you can think freely and without interruption. Make sure your writing pad is big enough so you can cover it with notes and ideas. You might want to use a newsprint pad or a whiteboard to give yourself plenty of thinking room. To start drawing your mind map, write a focus word or phrase like "Sales Volume" in the approximate center of the page. This is the key idea that starts the mind map. It is the trunk from which you start to branch out by verbal association. Draw a few short lines radiating outward like spokes from the key idea in the center.

Put yourself in a relaxed frame of mind and let your thoughts begin to spin. Free-associate your ideas with the key idea at the center. Start thinking of various questions, ideas, subtopics, facts, and related factors that branch out from the key idea. Begin writing these various associated ideas at the ends of the spokes so you can see how they connect to the key idea. Don't pause to think about any one subtopic in detail; just keep fanning out ideas of all kinds. Draw more radial spokes as you need them.

Using "Sales Volume" as your starting point, you might expand outward on the page and surround that term with such topics as: Leads, Cold Calling, Customer Lists, Commissions, Sales Training, Turnaround Time, Quotas, Incentives, Product Categories, Shipping Costs, Billing Procedures, Performance Evaluations, and Follow-Up Procedures (see Figure 12–1).

Each of the subtopics on your mind map might lead you to think of other sub-subtopics related to it. For example, Leads might break down further to Existing Leads, Ways of Getting New Leads, Qualifying Leads Better, and so on. Just draw other branching lines outward from Leads, and write the subordinate ideas at the ends of the lines. You can break the subject down to as many levels as you like. You will quickly see that the whole page is starting to look like a branching network of related ideas, something like a huge spiderweb. This is a mind map—a pictorial representation of what you know about a subject.

The point here is that you are more or less brainstorming on paper, but with a twist. Mind-mapping helps you to organize your ideas around a central theme. Whereas verbal brainstorming

FIGURE 12–1:   Mind Map

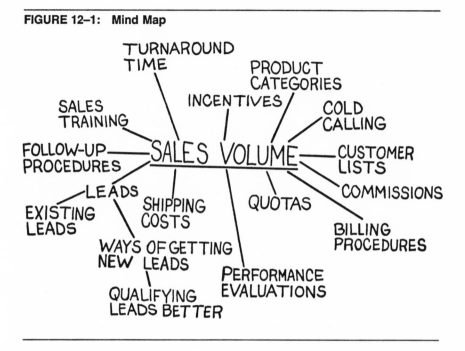

produces a list of ideas, mind-mapping produces a two-dimensional "sketch" of concepts that all relate to one another and to a central idea.

You will quickly discover that mind-mapping leads you to consider many topics and factors that might not otherwise have come to mind had you sat down and tried to make an outline or plan right away. Mind-mapping is a simple, yet powerful way to think conceptually and relationally. It is a method for organized divergent thinking. One idea suggests another. Each topic breaks down into subtopics. You never lose track of your objective because the mind map keeps everything together for you.

When you have thoroughly itemized the topics and subtopics that revolve around Sales Volume, and you have studied the whole mind map carefully, you can decide how to transform your two-dimensional picture of the problem into a one-dimensional report or plan. Each branch of the mind map represents a key concept you can put in your report and discuss with your colleagues. Some of the ideas on your mind map may not be as feasible as others, so you will have to prioritize your list. This is another benefit of using the mind map technique; it allows you to organize and prioritize your thoughts for a specific purpose.

An easy way to convert the mind map into an outline for a written report is to number the various major branches of the mind map in some logical sequence. These major branches can become major headings in your report or plan. The subbranches, of course, become subsections under the major headings. Then you can simply type out an outline and begin to write up the report.

The mind map, or "spidergram," as it is sometimes called, is one of the most powerful aids available to help you develop and use your conceptual thinking abilities. It is a creative thinking tool that helps you organize your thoughts around a central idea. Mind-mapping helps you to think globally and conceptually by putting you into a divergent, brainstorming mode.

EXECUTIVE MIND-MAPPING

Mind-mapping is also very effective in a group situation with a leader who is trained in CPS methods. In this instance, the leader uses an easel pad, a large piece of butcher paper, a chalkboard, or an erasable whiteboard as his or her "pad." From there, the leader elicits information, issues, facts, question topics, problems, and subproblems from the group, writing them on a mind map around the central idea. Each topic that surrounds the central idea then becomes its own central idea, with ideas shooting off from it.

The mind map is also a very effective method for executive planning retreats, as will be described later. Figure 12–2 is a photographic reduction of an actual mind map developed during an extensive planning retreat which I facilitated for a large power company. This particular mind map was one of a series we developed as we analyzed the company's business environment. It is reproduced exactly as it was drawn, with no attempt at artistic rendering. Rest assured that all the topics written on the mind map made sense to the executives involved, even though it might not be completely familiar to the casual observer. It is included here merely to exemplify the technique of mind-mapping.

We had first created a primary mind map that portrayed a breakdown of the various sectors of the company's environment in terms of categorical labels such as customer, competitor, eco-

FIGURE 12–2   A Typical Mind Map of Business Strategy

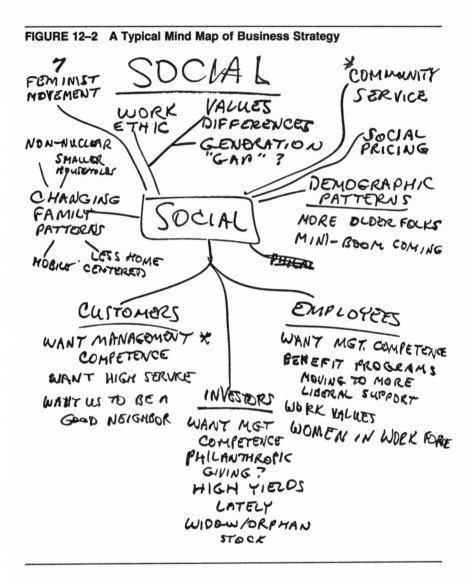

nomic, social, technical, political, legal, and physical. With the mind map shown, we were beginning to explore the various social factors we could think of that might have an impact on the company's business picture in the future. The topics shown led to a much more intensive discussion of various issues and subissues, again using the mind-mapping technique to keep the discussion and analysis manageable.

The mind-mapping technique is also quite effective as a method of note-taking. In a meeting situation, at a seminar, or while listening to a lecture, you can follow the most disorganized, rambling discussion by capitalizing on the two-dimensional feature of the mind map. Whereas the traditional method of taking notes requires that you write all of the information in a continuous column running down one page after another, the mind map allows you to use the entire two-dimensional writing surface to capture ideas and connect them.

You are not obliged to follow the sequence of the speakers or discussion participants. You can go all over the mind map if you like, tucking each new item of information into the branching structure as you see fit. When you have finished, you no longer have a rambling list of disconnected bits and pieces. Instead you have a coherent picture of the key ideas that have been discussed, with each shown in its proper relationship to the others.

Mind-mapping is not a word-for-word, verbatim note-taking technique. It involves grasping the gist of the speaker's point, not all the details. Mind-mapping works because it forces you to organize and prioritize the most important points of the session.

One other advantage is that the mind map can help you explain a difficult concept to a colleague. The wide-open look of the "spidergram" offers an easily recognizable format that others can understand. They can see each aspect of the project or idea you wish to discuss. This has a twofold impact because at the same time you can teach other people to use the mind map technique for themselves. This will help them express their ideas better in the future.

Use the mind map technique as often as you can. It takes some practice to become skilled at it. The purpose of the technique is to give you a natural way to think divergently, conceptually, and globally, while still keeping your attention fastened on the problem you set out to solve. You'll soon find yourself feeling much more fluent and comfortable with big-picture thinking, and much more able to influence the ideas of others.

CHAPTER THIRTEEN

Intellectual Courage

"The dissenter is every human being at those moments of his life when he resigns momentarily from the herd and thinks for himself."

ARCHIBALD MacLEISH

Intellectual courage is the willingness to advocate an idea or a course of action which you believe in, but which is unpopular with your peers. Some of the most famous thinkers in history were intellectually courageous, and some even lost their lives defending their views. The effective innovator needs a dash of intellectual courage to help him or her rise above the limiting assumptions and views of the surrounding culture.

MARCONI-ISM

Guglielmo Marconi, considered by many to be the father of modern radio, had a great deal of persistence. He tried for years to interest people in the potential of the new phenomenon of wireless communication as a way to put people in contact with one another over long distances. Yet his road to historical significance was not an easy one. When he explained the concept of radio waves to the public, fearful critics in the crowd wanted to hang him as a religious heretic. His father, convinced of the utter worthless nature of his "childish" pursuit, actually destroyed his son's first radio transmitting equipment.

Around the turn of the century, Marconi proposed that it might be possible to transmit radio signals back and forth between Europe and North America on a regular basis. Remember that the only form of intercontinental communication at that time was sea mail. No radio, no television, no satellites existed to carry telephone messages. It took many weeks at the very minimum to exchange messages between continents. Marconi was proposing to do it in seconds.

Most of the "experts" in electricity declared that Marconi's fantasy was impossible, even on a theoretical basis. They reasoned—quite correctly, with the available evidence—that the Earth's curvature would prevent the radio signal from reaching its destination. It would travel off into space many miles above the intended ground receiver.

Even though Marconi could not refute the theorists, he persisted in his investigations. In 1901 he succeeded in transmitting the Morse code letter *S* from Cornwall, England, to Newfoundland. Only later did physicists discover the *ionosphere*, an atmospheric layer of charged particles surrounding the Earth that has the effect of bending radio waves to cause them to follow the Earth's curvature.

Marconi was willing to put up with scorn, ridicule, and embarrassment from people who "knew" his idea would never work. He had the last laugh.

To commemorate Marconi's contribution as a role model for persistence, I have coined the term *Marconi-ism* in his honor. Marconi-ism is the act of persisting in a worthwhile course of action long enough to see it through.

HANNIBALISM

The famous Carthaginian general Hannibal had a great idea: he would use elephants in his battles with the Romans. The enormous animals would frighten the enemy, serve as armored mounts for his leaders, and help transport equipment. His escapades with the elephants were so newsworthy that Hannibal and his elephants are vaguely familiar to most educated people today.

In order to make the long and treacherous crossing of the Alps, Hannibal chose large elephants to carry his supplies. With a long line of elephants in tow, he journeyed to the battlefields of Italy. He believed the elephants would also make excellent fighting animals.

Unfortunately, the elephants were an unqualified disaster. The huge beasts couldn't navigate the slippery roads through the mountains and became unmanageable at the high altitudes. They were also a liability rather than an asset on the battlefield because the tremendous din and clamor of the fighting frightened them. Many of the huge animals turned and stampeded, trampling Hannibal's soldiers in the process. If you had been one of his foot soldiers, the prospect of being run over by an enormous, terrified pachyderm would have given you a different slant on military elephants than Hannibal had.

Yet Hannibal never gave up on his conviction that the elephant was a military innovation of great potential. In fact, on his death-bed he is said to have declared, "I could have beaten them [the Romans] if I'd only had more elephants."

To commemorate Hannibal's contribution as a role model for persistence, I have coined the term *Hannibalism* in his honor. Hannibalism is the act of persisting with an idea that doesn't pay off, long after the evidence is clear.

MARCONI-ISM OR HANNIBALISM: WHICH IS IT?

One of the more interesting paradoxes in the consideration of intellectual courage is how to tell the difference between Marconi-ism and Hannibalism. The big question is: "How do you know which is which?" What *is* the difference between intellectual courage and pigheadedness? The dictionary defines pigheadedness as "being stupidly obstinate about something." Intellectual courage is fighting for what you believe in, and pigheadedness is not knowing when to quit. How do you know when you're being intellectually courageous and when you're being pigheaded?

The distinction is an important one. It's just as important to know when to change direction and try something else as it is to stick to your guns. When does Marconi-ism become Hannibalism? When is it time to quit, and when is it best to continue to struggle along to the end? Remember that Thomas Edison tried over 700 different materials for his light bulb filament. What made him go on instead of throwing in the towel? What made him consider new ideas instead of retrying things he knew wouldn't work? Why did Marconi continue to work, even after his friends, family, and peers scorned him? On the other hand, what prevented Hannibal from reconsidering his obsession with the elephants?

Hard work and effort toward the wrong aim is useless. The trick to being intellectually courageous is to know when you are wasting your time and when you need to press on to the end.

Yet this is not an easy thing to know. There is an inescapable element of personal judgment involved. Let's examine some case histories in intellectual courage to see what common threads might exist.

PROFILES IN INTELLECTUAL COURAGE

Attacking creativity and creative thinkers is not new. Through all of history we can see many examples of men and women who faced criticism and continued to march in their chosen direction. Alexander Graham Bell, Albert Einstein, the Wright brothers, George Washington Carver, Henry David Thoreau, George Washington, and Abraham Lincoln are examples of people who exhibited intellectual courage in the face of critical appraisal.

Many women in history have added their own brand of intellectual courage in the face of role stereotypes as well as narrow thinking. Madame Marie Curie, Florence Nightingale, and Eleanor Roosevelt were all intelligent, talented, and courageous women who not only had to overcome their own individual problems but also the hatred and derision of some of their male counterparts.

Madame Curie faced several problems throughout her scientific career. Her critics doubted her theories as a scientist, not because she may have been wrong but largely because she was a woman. Even after winning a number of awards from the scientific community for her work with radioactive materials, she still failed to gain the acceptance of her male peers. She never let this problem interfere with her innovative mind and continued to make important scientific contributions until she died.

Thomas Jefferson, George Washington, Benjamin Franklin, and John Hancock are seen as founding fathers of our country. Their skillful and courageous work on such documents as the Declaration of Independence and Constitution led to our present system of government. They are popular men today, but their ideas frequently went against the intellectual current of their times. The decisions leading up to the Revolutionary War were not popular with many colonialist leaders who did not want to antagonize Britain. Jefferson and the others stood their ground in the face of this criticism and presented their views dramatically to King George III.

Florence Nightingale spent much of her life working with the sick and injured. She was in charge of 24 other British nurses caring for injured soldiers during the Crimean War. The founder of modern nursing as we know it faced the chauvinistic scorn of her male counterparts who told her women "had no place doing doctors' work." Her knowledge of medicine and a calm bedside manner helped move the art and science of medicine into the modern world.

Charles Darwin's theory of natural selection stood up against the criticisms of a number of disbelieving scholars. His critics could not accept his theory because of its apparent opposition to the biblical theory of creation. Darwin backed his theory with a tremendous amount of research. While his innovative theories and research methods were not immediately appreciated by other naturalists, he eventually prevailed.

Henry David Thoreau was a naturalist and philosopher whose writing led to the development of such political strategies as civil disobedience. His views were often controversial, and he was not well liked in the philosophical community. Yet his teachings provided the basis for many of the views of modern leaders like Martin Luther King, Jr.

Abraham Lincoln was president of the United States during an extremely turbulent time. His views on the Civil War and the volatile topic of slavery made him a very unpopular man with many people. He showed his courage to his critics publicly through both the Gettysburg Address and the Emancipation Proclamation. He was a lonely man in many ways, but he charted his course and pursued it unwaveringly.

Alexander Graham Bell is recognized as the pioneer of the modern telephone. Yet even as he proved the value of his invention, he faced many, many skeptics. Many people thought the telephone was a hoax, and not really an actual long-distance communication device at all. Bell stuck to his guns and proved the value of his invention. Today we use the telephone on a daily basis and think nothing of the time, energy, and effort that went into its design and implementation.

Almost everyone has heard the story of the Wright brothers' famous flight. Imagine the ridicule and criticism heaped on them as they tested their airplane. Think about the number of times they heard the phrase "It'll never work." Still they pressed on, undaunted by the skeptics who knew for certain that the plane would never leave the ground. Up until the day of the Wright brothers' historic trip, heavier-than-air winged flight was thought to be impossible. In a few short minutes they proved it was both possible and reliable through their vision and courage.

Even after Thomas Edison's reputation as an inventor was known worldwide, he felt the heat of scorn from a host of doubters who thought he was wasting his time. "What good is it?" a skeptical politician once asked Edison at a demonstration of his new light bulb. "Well, one day you'll be able to tax it," was the inventor's acidic reply.

Albert Einstein is thought of as a great scientist. Yet his early theories were often ridiculed by his colleagues in the scientific community. His often disheveled appearance and forgetful tendency made him an easy target for local idea killers. Yet his intellect and, more important, his intellectual courage strengthened his philosophy and gave credence to his ideas. By sheer force of intellect, he won worldwide respect and admiration. Einstein was also a dedicated pacifist, a role which earned him the intense animosity of a number of people. He advocated the formation of a single world government that would be superior to all governments, including that of the United States, his adopted country.

Eleanor Roosevelt carved out her own reputation even though the work of her famous husband had captured the limelight. Her work with the underprivileged and poor won her a great deal of respect. Her sharp wit and strong sense of determination earned her a reputation as an intellectual in her own right.

Mohandas K. Gandhi and Martin Luther King, Jr., believed in using nonviolent civil disobedience to achieve their goals. Gandhi used long periods of fasting to dramatize his beliefs. King often made speeches to the masses and participated in peaceful protest marches. Both men abhorred violence, although it often flared up around them. Yet even in the face of danger and contempt, they were inspiring and eloquent, confronting bigoted critics and standing their ground in the face of intense hatred and anger. Because of their beliefs and the enormous impact of those beliefs on others, both men lost their lives to assassins.

Pablo Picasso, the famous painter, antagonized many of the early critics of his works. His peculiar abstract, impressionistic paintings were passed over by art experts who did not care for his ideas or methods. Yet today his paintings bring high prices at auctions, and he is classified as one of the world's greatest painters. Picasso proved that he could "sell" his imaginative painting techniques to the critics and the public. Whatever you personally may think of his paintings, he was an innovative and creative man—one who captured his visions in his works.

Robert Goddard and Wernher von Braun were two scientists who contributed significantly to the philosophy and direction of the American space program. Goddard was virtually the founding father of modern rocketry, and von Braun implemented many of the plans that led to the Apollo moon landings. In the early days of rocketry, there were 10 critics for every contributor. Some thought it was impossible to fly a rocket beyond the Earth's orbit. Others believed that while it might be possible to do so, it would be a waste of time, talent, and money. Still others even thought such an effort was immoral.

Both men had the foresight and the persistence to continue their research for many years. Von Braun lived to see the triumph of a safe and successful moon landing. Goddard did not. When science writer Isaac Asimov was asked what words he would consider fitting for the first astronaut to say as he stepped onto the moon, he replied immediately, "Goddard, we are here."

Comedian Lenny Bruce was often labeled a malcontent and an unnecessarily profane entertainer. Yet his work has inspired many of today's most popular performers, including Woody Allen, Richard Pryor, Robin Williams, and George Carlin. Bruce's monologues were often heavy with obscenity, but not just for the sake of being obscene. His performances made a social statement, criticizing the double standards and inequities in our culture—its language, thoughts, and behavior. He frequently stretched the accepted limits on the public use of language and free speech, even going to jail in support of his belief in his material. Whether you liked him or not, he was an innovative and creative performer who upset the status quo of his time.

R. Buckminster Fuller had many talents. All his adult life he was an inventor, engineer, architect, poet, and stargazer. Most important, he was a creative thinker. Fuller was responsible for the invention and implementation of over 170 patented ideas, including the famous geodesic dome. The author of 24 books, he made 57 trips aound the world, sharing his never-ending supply of ideas with others.

As a young man, Fuller was expelled from Harvard in his freshman year. Yet this did not dampen his enthusiasm or creativity, and he often would spend up to 22 hours a day studying math, architecture, and physics. His ability to put his creative ideas into practice made him the leading innovator of futuristic products. He was often branded a kook because his ideas seemed so impossible at the time. Criticism had little effect on him, and he continued to create new inventions right up until his death.

THE DIFFERENCE BETWEEN COURAGE AND PIGHEADEDNESS

The difference between being intellectually courageous and being pigheaded is really just a matter of judgment. When you have embarked on an important idea venture and are following a course of action you believe to be worthwhile, you may not have any ironclad evidence that you are right. You are proceeding on the basis of your conviction. Others may believe you are wrong, but you believe you are right. If you could prove conclusively that you were right, there would be no need for intellectual courage in the face of opposition or censure.

When your venture is in its most discouraging phase and you have to proceed on the strength of your conviction, you still need to be open to the possibility that you might be making a mistake. Your idea might not really work, after all. You won't know until the end of the venture whether you are right. So intellectual courage boils down to a combination of faith in yourself and good judgment. Here are three things you can do to steer a reasonable course between giving up too soon and being pigheaded.

1. *Have faith in yourself.* Let your own knowledge, judgment, and opinions outrank those of the people around you. Set up a filter in your mind that screens out all but the most expert, highly qualified opinions about the feasibility or desirability of your undertaking. During the darkest hours of the Civil War, Abraham Lincoln remarked, "If I turn out to be right, it won't matter who agreed with me. If I'm wrong, a thousand angels pleading my case in Heaven won't make any difference either."

2. *Don't take advice from "sidewalk superintendents."* Motivational speaker Charles "Tremendous" Jones says, "I don't want advice from anybody who hasn't done what I'm trying to do and paid the price I'm willing to pay." The famous playwright Lillian

Hellman once remarked, "The best advice I can give a young writer is to not listen to advice from other writers."

3. *Reconsider your theory occasionally.* Be willing to question your basic premise at certain points along the way to make sure you are facing reality accurately. But don't let feelings of discouragement interfere with an objective reconsideration of your goal. If you are feeling down, discouraged, and fatigued, that's no time to rethink your purposes. Do your rethinking when you feel rested and optimistic. As Davy Crockett said, "Be sure you're right; then go ahead."

CHAPTER FOURTEEN

Creativity and Self-Confidence

"Change your thoughts and you change your world."

NORMAN VINCENT PEALE

One of the most common blocks to creative thinking can be a simple lack of self-confidence. People who don't think very highly of themselves often feel that while other people may have good ideas, they themselves are incapable of being creative. If your self-concept does not include the right to be creative, perhaps you need to do some creative thinking about your self-concept.

Your self-concept or self-image is a set of ideas that you have about yourself. These conscious and unconscious notions define you as a person in your own mind, in terms of your sense of self-esteem, your worthiness, and your capabilities. Some parts of your self-concept are positive and helpful while others may be negative and not so helpful.

HOW YOU FORMED YOUR SELF-CONCEPT

When you first popped out of the womb, you began the process of becoming a person. You began the long journey of figuring out how to "make it" in the world. You learned to cry for food, to signal in primitive ways for your other needs, and to get feelings of comfort and protection.

As you grew older and became a functioning individual, you began to integrate into your conscious and unconscious mental processes an understanding of what it took to survive, get feelings of security, and get love and attention from others. You kept those tactics that worked for you, that is, got you what you wanted and evaded what you didn't want, and you abandoned those tactics that were unsuccessful. You formed a set of *coping mechanisms* or habits that enabled you to get along the best you knew how.

While you were working out the puzzle of successful behavior and having that behavior shaped into a consistent pattern that became your personality, you were also working out—largely unconsciously—a theory of who you were. You assembled, through a slow and sometimes painful process, a collection of inputs that led you to assess and evaluate yourself in terms of your worth as a person. You learned to compare yourself with others and with the expectations others had for you.

When you were in the earliest stages of your growth, you realized that the big people (most likely your parents) controlled your life. They had all the power, they made the world run, and they made the rules. You reacted to their stimuli as virtually your only source of information about yourself. Your personal conclusions about yourself as a human being came almost entirely from these regular encounters. Your parents, grandparents, and other relatives and friends who helped your growth were probably not professional psychologists; they were amateurs in the subject of child development. They raised you the best they knew how.

When the big people were kind to you, praised you, petted you, protected you, and loved you, you felt good. You felt worthwhile and wanted. You concluded, at least partially, that you were a valued and valuable person.

When they scolded you, punished you, rejected you, or put you down, you felt bad. You concluded, again partially, that you were not a valuable person. Through both these experiences you formed your concept of yourself in terms of what you were worth, especially compared to the evaluations of others.

The most important thing to understand about your self-concept is this:

You formed your self-concept out of the value judgments the big people communicated to you.

You were constantly getting value messages from people in your environment, and you were interpreting those messages in terms of your own worth as a person. As an adult, the self-concept you have is largely a relic of the concept you had of yourself when you came out of adolescence and entered your early growing-up phase. Unless you have consciously reviewed that self-concept and revised it for the better, you may very likely be carrying around in the back of your mind an unnecessarily negative image of yourself, formed from obsolete data.

"Zips" and "Zaps"

From the moment you are born until you die, you experience countless microepisodes that shape your behavior. Some of them are positive for you, others are negative, but most are in between. Positive episodes or "zips" are those that cause you to feel safe, secure, confident, physically pleasurable, content, happy, cared for, cared about, and loved. Negative episodes or "zaps" are those that cause you to feel afraid, insecure, physically painful, sad, angry, uncared-for, and unloved. People are very often the sources of zips and zaps, but not always.

Just like any other animal, your behavior and reactions are shaped and conditioned by these positive and negative episodes, these zips and zaps. When you were a child you might have been burned when you touched a hot stove. This unpleasant experience registered itself permanently in your brain. You learned that touching a hot stove was a painful and unpleasant experience, a zap. As you experienced more and more zaps, you learned about more and more things to stay away from.

Most psychologists believe that we human beings start out in childhood as outgoing, gregarious, love-seeking, exploring creatures, but that we get zapped in so many ways that we shrink back to the basic patterns of behavior that we can safely trust. We abandon the more risky patterns because we don't want to get hurt any more.

As you collect your zips and zaps, you are continually posting entries to an unconscious ledger in your brain. You are *interpreting* the zips and zaps as well as having your behavior shaped by them. Your interpretation is a *conclusion* (at a micro level) about yourself, in terms of "how good a person you are."

Understanding Your Current Self-Concept

Think of your self-concept or your self-image as defined in your mind in terms of three factors:

1. *What you're lovable for.* Those characteristics you have that you believe induce people to care for you; what you have to do to get people to love you.
2. *What you're capable of.* An evaluative profile of your skills, abilities, talents, and potential for success; what you believe you are "good at," and what you believe you are "no good at."
3. *What you're worthy of.* Your merit as an individual; your sense of rights and entitlement in dealing with other people; how you are valued as a person.

Your own sense of lovability, capability, and worthiness are the three most powerful areas of influence for the health, growth, and development of your self-concept. The problem most people have is that they don't consider themselves to be lovable, capable, and worthy all at the same time.

Note that the terms *lovability, capability,* and *worthiness* are not objective characteristics like hair color and height. The zips and zaps you've received have led you to make *assumptions* about your lovability, capability, and worth that guide your present behavior.

Some people feel fairly lovable and capable, but not very worthy. They have difficulty seeing themselves as important. A person may not feel deserving of a top sales award or a promotion because deep down inside, he or she hears a voice that says, "You don't really deserve this." This sense of unworthiness can manifest itself in strong feelings of self-doubt that can hold a person back from achieving realistic goals. Some people actually even "sabotage" their own plans because of this feeling of low worth.

Other people feel capable and worthy, but not very lovable. They believe they cannot love someone or receive love in return. They may go from one person to another in search of true love. Inability to accept love from someone has a lot to do with feelings of negative self-worth, too.

Still other people may feel lovable and worthwhile, but not very capable. These people may have little faith in their capabilities as workers, thinkers, or even as human beings engaged in the ordinary logistical matters of living. If you have a demanding job and make frequent mistakes at it, you may begin to feel like you aren't a very capable worker. This can cause you to perform even more poorly as these feelings increase.

It is important to realize that a large portion of your self-concept formed itself before you learned your language skills. For that reason, much of your self-concept is nonverbal or preverbal, in that it exists as a set of feeling reactions connected to the memories of various concrete experiences. This is why you might find yourself getting angry, hurt, guilty, or defensive in some situation and not knowing exactly why. You are reacting to an ancient trace in your brain that links a programmed feeling response to an event you are re-experiencing.

Because the self-concept is largely unconscious and preverbal, it is difficult for many people to be objective and accurate about how they see themselves. There is a big temptation to rationalize one's behavior and delude oneself into the artificial belief that one is a confident, well-rounded person and to reject the facts of one's feelings and behavior.

A SELF-CONCEPT QUIZ

Here is a short quiz to help you identify any behavior patterns you may have that might indicate unconscious negative assumptions about yourself as a person. Beside each of the following questions, write a number from 1 to 5, which you feel best describes your actions, reactions, or behavior in most cases.

Use the following scale: 1 = seldom or never true of me; 2 = usually not true of me; 3 = sometimes true of me; 4 = usually true of me; and 5 = almost always true of me.

When you have finished, add up all the values to get a grand total and subtract the grand total from 100 to get a positively oriented score. The final number is a numerical assessment of your own self-esteem and self-concept. As you take the quiz, try to keep in mind how you will answer the questions in terms of both your personal life and your business life. Be as honest and objective about yourself as possible.

SELF-CONCEPT QUIZ

1. I usually describe myself in derogatory terms, ones that suggest I am physically unattractive, undesirable, or otherwise unlovable.
2. I am uncomfortable and unsure of myself when I meet new people.
3. I "show off" at parties, social gatherings, or other group functions in order to get attention.
4. I find it difficult to seek affection from another person.
5. I allow other people to make me feel guilty.
6. I like to take advantage of my position of authority and use any opportunity to get "one up" on other people.
7. I enjoy putting people in their places.
8. I describe myself in derogatory terms—ones that suggest I am inept, unintelligent, untalented, or otherwise incapable.
9. I avoid taking risks in most of my activities. I seldom try anything new if I'm not completely sure that I can do it.
10. I have very few goals that I am actively trying to accomplish.
11. I get defensive if someone says or implies that I haven't done something properly or effectively.
12. I am moody and tend to react strongly to the things that other people say and do.
13. I describe myself in derogatory terms—ones that suggest I am unimportant, insignificant, or otherwise unworthy of respect and consideration of others.
14. I get embarrassed or uncomfortable when other people praise me or compliment me. I typically deny that I've done anything worthy of praise.
15. I let other people take advantage of me. I don't insist on my rights when other people violate them.
16. I am easily intimidated by other people.
17. I feel uncomfortable, inferior, and unsure of myself when I'm around people in authority.
18. I find it difficult to speak up in meetings or other group situations.
19. I like to intimidate other people and make them feel small, stupid, or otherwise inferior to me.
20. I like to let other people know I've "made it" by the car I drive and the clothes I wear.

Total = _____   100 minus Total = _____

How did you score? Did you discover anything new about the way you perceive yourself? Look at this chart of numbers that explain your score:

0–25: Very negative self-concept
25–50: Negative self-concept

50–75: Weak-to-moderate self-concept

75–100: Positive self-concept

Reread the questions one by one and see which of them pertain most to each of the three aspects of self-concept, lovability, capability, and worthiness. Do you find one of these three factors stronger in yourself than the others? Which one do you feel is lowest for you?

DEFINING YOUR FEELINGS

Negative experiences that make you feel bad about yourself are often the result of a specific stimulus. This is often linked to negative stimuli that helped form your self-concept.

Do certain things get your goat easily? Can someone say a certain thing, use a certain term, or speak to you in a certain way and reliably get a rise out of you? These actions or events are *grabbers*—things other people can say or do to trigger negative emotions.

Grabbers can be *trigger words* to which you might react angrily or defensively, such as: stupid, fat, girl, boy, kid, or any slur against your ethnic, national, or racial origins. Grabbers can throw off your positive feelings. Some people who enjoy putting others down may throw these grabbers at you to hit what they may know are your emotional soft spots.

One way to strengthen your self-concept is to identify when and how you react to grabbers. The quiz offered one way to identify your problem areas, but the best way is to take a pen and a sheet of paper and make a list of grabbers that affect you the most.

Think of the times in your life when you felt the most unsure of yourself. Try to analyze why the grabbers made you feel the way you did. Some of them might have hit on your emotional states and caused feelings like fear, anger, apprehension, guilt, embarrassment, or anxiety. When you feel uncentered and unsure of yourself as a human being, you are responding to something that makes you feel incapable, unlovable, and unworthy.

Certain threatening social situations, office encounters, and complex problem-solving episodes can bring on these feelings of self-doubt. Try to recognize the specific situations and the specific stimuli that cause you to have these feelings. Ask yourself, "Why do I feel incapable in this situation? What makes me feel unloved? What am I reacting to that makes me feel I'm not a very worthwhile person?"

As an example, you may feel incapable of completing a complex project for your boss. Maybe you feel that you lack the necessary skills or that you may fail in your efforts.

Maybe you feel that you are not a lovable person. This can hinder your dealings with the opposite sex. You may feel that there is no "right" person in this world for you. This lack of self-confidence makes you feel alone in a crowded social environment.

As another example, you may have worked at a company for several years. You feel that you should receive a pay raise, but you don't have the courage to ask your boss for it. Here you may harbor certain feelings of doubt about your worthiness. You cannot bring yourself to ask for a raise because maybe deep down inside you may feel you really don't deserve one.

In each case your negative self-concept can interfere with your life. We all have these types of problems in one form or another. It is important to recognize the negative impact of these episodes as they occur. If you can understand why you feel inadequate, you can begin to change the way you think about yourself. Remember that each time you feel inadequate about yourself, it is probably because you feel incapable, unloved, or unworthy.

We all have a soft spot or two in one or more of these areas. No one is completely free from these feelings now and then. However, the most creative, innovative, and inventive people can work around these difficulties by realizing that, above all, they are lovable, capable, and worthwhile.

One of the biggest problems related to these so-called soft spots is that people who recognize them in you may try to take advantage of them. When other people discover these sensitive areas that relate to your lovability, capability, and worth, they may sometimes try to manipulate you for their own benefit by using zaps and grabbers.

DEALING WITH THE ZAPPERS

Some people are zappers. Because of their own low self-esteem they get their power feelings by trying to make others feel small. Some zappers have a tendency to target their potshots specifically at your soft spots. The zapper may learn that you feel especially vulnerable in group or social situations because you feel you are not very worthwhile. In this type of situation, the zapper may hide in the weeds waiting for his or her chance to strike. If you decide to introduce a new thought or concept to the group, the zapper may take the opportunity to put you down by hitting at your feelings of self-doubt.

How you react to the criticism from a zapper is critical to your positive self-concept. As a rule, people usually respond to attacks on their soft spots in one of two distinct ways: capitulation or compensation.

People who harbor doubts about their own abilities or their worthiness often choose the route of capitulation. They don't like to make waves, they dislike confrontations, and they try to avoid risks. When the zapper fires a shot, the capitulator backs down and gives in to the aggressive behavior.

The compensator, on the other hand, reacts in a very different way from the capitulator. The compensator masks his or her feelings of low self-worth by an aggressive display of energy. A loud voice, a domineering pattern of speech, fierce looks, and the nonverbal patterns of power and dominance are this person's weapons to keep others from knowing how weak and insignificant he or she actually feels.

Compensators deceive themselves by hiding their feelings of inadequacy behind a fake front. These people try to project a false bravado, hiding behind a mask of apparent self-confidence and assuredness. They often talk loudly, forcefully, or aggressively, and use so-called pressure tactics to help themselves feel more powerful and important. Put simply, while the capitulator behaves rather passively, the compensator behaves rather aggressively. Which of the two styles best describes your own personal behavior? That of your friends or colleagues? Do you recognize compensation traits in people you identify as zappers?

Neither of these behaviors is effective for improving your own sense of self-worth. They both involve a form of defeat, a feeling that you cannot fight for what you believe in without either giving up or using aggressive behavior to get other people to give in.

Capitulation and compensation patterns are generally negative and self-defeating. If you are a capitulator, you need to forcefully reorganize your self-concept to meet the challenges of the zappers in the world. If you are a compensator, you need to identify the reasons that make you feel as if you must do battle with other people most of the time. Concentrate on the more positive sides of your personality. Move to a higher level of your own self-concept by redefining the opinion you hold of yourself.

Recognize the fact that idea killing is just another form of zapping. If you can spot certain zapper statements that are designed to irritate you or throw you off your positive track, then you won't personalize the attack the next time you see it. You can take yourself off the hook for the emotions tied to each zapper statement. A strong self-concept is one that projects the message "I am lovable, capable, and worthy." This tells the zapper that his or her grabbers don't affect you.

REORGANIZING YOUR SELF-CONCEPT

If you are to grow as a person, you must have a positive feeling for yourself. Once you reassess yourself unconditionally as a lovable, capable, and worthy person, you lay claim to all that is due you in life. Analyze your own self-concept and try to understand which situations give you the most trouble. When you encounter a situation that makes you feel unlovable, incapable, or not worthy, stop and tell yourself that you are indeed lovable, capable, worthwhile, and more.

Here is a powerful thought that deals with positive thinking and your ability to get what you want out of life. It's been attributed to many different people, and it sums up a way to perceive your goals in terms of your self-concept:

If it's possible in the world, it's possible for you. It's only a question of how.

Take this statement to heart. If what you want to do is humanly possible in our world, then it can be done, and you can be the one to do it. If you have faith in yourself and the energy to put behind your ideas, then you can do whatever you want to do.

As I mentioned in Chapter Ten, it also helps to become highly conscious of your language habits, especially with regard to the way you talk about yourself. Be very careful what you say after you say the words "I am." Whatever you say in this sense is something you are beginning to make true. Detect the negative self-descriptions that you may frequently use and eliminate them from your conversations. Say positive things about yourself, and they will become true.

Use positive self-programming as another self-concept builder. Tell yourself every time you go to bed and every time you wake up, "I am a lovable, capable, and worthy person."

CHAPTER FIFTEEN

Team Creativity

"It is not who is right, but what is right that counts."

THOMAS HUXLEY

A creative team is one in which all the members can collaborate effectively to develop superior solutions to the problems they undertake. Whether it is an organizational work unit, a task force, or a special committee, the creative team works by synergy. Each member can contribute ideas and energy to the goal of solving the problem.

Ineffective teams waste time, resources, and energy, and their solutions are often mediocre or ineffective. Creative teams achieve effective solutions, and they do it with a smaller investment of time, energy, and resources.

When the members of a team are skilled in creative problem-solving (CPS) methods, their solutions are virtually always superior to those of any individual working alone. Thus the role of creative teamwork in an organization is potentially powerful.

TEAM SYNERGY

An often-repeated demonstration of the potential of team synergy is the well-known "NASA Moon Exercise." This problem requires group members to prioritize their goals on the basis of certain criteria. The group is given this scenario: "You have landed on the moon. You have taken a separate craft to explore the other side of the moon; unfortunately, it has crashed and is beyond repair. You have a list of 15 specific items salvaged from your craft, and you need to decide what to take with you. You must rank the provisions in the order of their importance—that is, on the basis of how useful they will be to you in your efforts to get back to your ship."

The items involved include a magnetic compass, signal flares, ropes, containers of water, a rubber life raft, oxygen bottles, and various tools.

This problem and its solution provide an excellent example of the impact of team creativity. Tests using the problem in both individual and team efforts showed some interesting conclusions. To set a standard for the problem, a group of NASA scientists ranked the items in terms of their usefulness on the moon. This list is used as a standard expert solution in evaluating the results produced by groups undertaking this exercise during CPS seminars and team-building workshops.

In nearly every case when the problem was given to individuals separately and subsequently to the same people in teams, the groups achieved far better results than did the individuals by themselves. The group rankings of the necessary provisions were always closer to the items on the standard expert list than the individual rankings.

The Power of the Group

Collaboration, meaning to "co-labor," involves working together in a special way. By communicating clearly, using option thinking, and getting access to all the needed information, a group can work together as a powerful unit to solve a wide variety of problems. When used skillfully, CPS techniques help the members of a group, committee, or task force handle information effectively, consider all of the available information, and come to a decision based on their collective knowledge. One of the keys to success is in knowing how and when to apply group problem-solving techniques. If you've ever participated in this type of activity, you probably had a profound sense of the difference between team problem-solving activities and individual problem-solving activities.

Ineffective groups working on certain projects usually have no clear sense of the outcome they want to achieve. Because they are not sure about their objective, they usually sit around and ramble on about the subject. They waste valuable time and do not get anywhere at all. Members seem to get wrapped up in the details they want to discuss and often lose sight of what they should be doing. Instead of developing an agenda, they tend to wander off the track and get distracted by irrelevant factors or issues.

Such groups frequently fall into adversary situations, and a difference of opinion or even an argument may break out between people or factions. As a result, the meeting often deteriorates into seeing who will win the battle. The person with the loudest voice or the highest rank often "wins" the argument and is able to control the meeting.

In the end, however, no one in the group actually "wins" anything. After the ego battling is over, few of the group members will feel like working on the problem anymore. Those involved in the fighting may leave with hurt feelings. The other more passive members may not want to continue the discussion. Bad feelings and side taking do little to foster effective solutions.

The Danger of Groupthink

A curious psychological phenomenon seems to dominate a great many of the thinking processes that go on in business meetings. This is the phenomenon of *premature closure*, in which members of the group switch too soon into a convergent thinking mode and jump at a particular conclusion, usually under the influence of a few strong personalities.

Psychologist Irving Janis coined the term *groupthink* to explain this psychological event. It results, says Janis, from insufficient awareness on the part of the group that they are engaged in the *process* of making a decision.[1]

According to the theory of groupthink, most of us place such a high value on convergent thinking and consensus and have so little confidence in our own thinking abilities that we tend to accept the points of view, opinions, and courses of actions proposed by individuals who speak out the loudest or with the most authority—whether or not those individuals know what they are talking about. We unconsciously allow ourselves to be herded into agreement.

This premature closure or changeover from divergent thinking to convergent thinking signals the end of problem exploration and option thinking, if indeed the group has engaged at all in such activity. The essence of the groupthink problem is this key transition and the enforcement of it by the most vocal members of a group.

What sometimes passes for group problem solving really amounts to a battle of wills between two people or two factions—a shouting match over who is right and who is wrong. Groupthink and all the other factors mentioned above usually cause group members to neglect many important ramifications of the problem at hand. Consequently, their solutions tend to be mundane, unimaginative, and frequently not very workable. They have really not thought through the problem well enough to come up with a mature and effective solution.

Everything that can be said about an effective individual problem solver can also be said about teams in a collective sense. But there is one major improvement: the team should always be better than one individual because of the synergy; the contribution of each individual enhances that of the others.

How the Creative Team Works

The number one factor in the success of team creativity is the simple but profoundly important skill of *process awareness*. One of the keys to a team's creative success is how effectively its members manage their own interaction processes instead of becoming preoccupied about the "content," that is, the subject at hand or the problem they are dealing with. In order to function well as a group, the members must develop some ground rules that will help them work together. These rules include things like agreeing on roles, learning to disagree without fighting, learning to process information as a unit, focusing their energies on specific outcomes, and committing themselves to concrete plans.

This is the basis of the *process-content distinction*. Members of a creative team must understand the difference between the process, that is, how you go about solving the problem, and the content or specific nature of the problem itself. Content is *what* you're doing and process is *how* you're doing it.

Probably only 15 or 20 percent of businesspeople have developed the skill of process awareness. Most people who work ineffectively in group settings miss the entire idea. They are too distracted by the content of the problem. People who are good take-over specialists in a group environment are masters of the process. They can watch the group and over a short period of time take certain steps to put the group back into a problem-solving mode after it has stalled because of some process malfunction, such as bickering over roles, blaming, arguing, or engaging in groupthink. The people in the group will usually tend to unconsciously elect these process-skilled people to informal roles of leadership or influence.

The real fun begins when all the members of a team share the process awareness skill. In this case people don't vie for the upper hand, either consciously or unconsciously. They all contribute their skills and knowledge to making the process effective. They continually evaluate a number of important factors: the information flow among themselves, their decision-making processes; the way they communicate with each other and bring up issues; how they maintain social rapport; and how they work on an entire problem.

THE IMPORTANCE OF THINKING
ABOUT THINKING

Part of the skill of process awareness is the ability of people to use both the divergent and convergent thinking skills described in Chapter Seven. When creative thinkers think divergently, they do it skillfully, not in a random or undisciplined way. They are not "off in the ozone." Divergent thinking is not a process of aimless wandering. It is a *managed process of thought* that explores, enlarges, and examines an issue before coming up with a solution.

When creative people think convergently, they get down to brass tacks by evaluating the possible solutions and coming up with an effective choice.

The creative team starts with a clear sense of purpose. Even if the problem they are attacking is only vaguely understood, the team members at least know which problem they are trying to solve and what outcome they are hoping for. They are willing to set aside or defer their judgments and deal with facts and issues. They see no sense in doing battle or arguing with someone who has a different point of view. They want to know the facts at hand and ask themselves, "What can I do to solve the problem without letting my personal feelings get in the way?"

Creative thinkers are comfortable in exploring a wide range of considerations and relevant factors. They have the ability to digest and grasp new information. They can arrange the new information into viable options instead of lunging at any handy solution.

Effective and creative thinkers have a special respect for evidence. They prefer to make decisions on the basis of correct information rather than argument. They are willing to investigate rather than rely on hearsay or other suspect information.

Creative teams are often well versed in specific CPS methods, such as brainstorming, information structuring, modeling, mindmapping (as described in Chapter Twelve), and other ways to share ideas about the problem at hand. They use these methods freely and easily and are comfortable with the logistics of managed thought and conscious problem solving.

BRAINSTORMING

The term *brainstorming* is now a familiar buzzword in the business community. Even though the term is popular, its usage is not. Many people pay lip service to the term but don't actually know how to do brainstorming. The brainstorming method is a very specific, well-defined process for producing ideas. Many people use the term loosely and nonspecifically. For example, an executive might say, "I want you to get a few people together and 'brainstorm' this problem. Give me a recommendation." What he or she probably means in most situations is, "Get together and argue out a course of action you can all live with."

The real brainstorming process is a very disciplined group-dynamic method based on specific rules. Pioneered by advertising executive Alex Osborn, the technique involves a group leader asking a group to solve a particular problem.[2] Throughout the problem-solving process the group leader enforces two rules: (1) the group will attempt to produce a large quantity of ideas; and (2) no one is allowed to evaluate any of the ideas offered during the brainstorming session.

The group members have only one goal: to produce as many ideas for solving the stated problem as possible. Their leader keeps them on track by not allowing comments about any of the ideas until after the session is complete. This allows the group members to speak freely and contribute as much as possible without fear of criticism. The leader can help the group members with suggestions if they get stalled around a certain part of the problem.

As you can see, this technique asks for a *quantity* of ideas; it is not concerned with quality at first. The participants are encouraged to generate as many ideas as they can in a rapid-fire fashion. No time is wasted debating the pros and cons of any one idea. All advocacy is postponed until the idea-producing session is finished and the evaluation process begins. This encourages the group members to free-associate with the problem so as to come up with a novel solution that may not have been considered previously.

The advantages of this technique in group work can also prove useful for you as an individual thinker. You can use the same techniques to generate ideas and possible solutions to your own specific problems. Once you have clearly stated the problem in your own mind, take a sheet of paper and a pen and begin to write down *everything* that comes to your mind as a possible option for solving it.

Now is not the time to evaluate what you are writing down—that will come later. The object is to generate a large quantity of ideas in a relatively brief period of time. Once you have exhausted all the possibilities you can think of, then go back and carefully analyze your work. You may discover that the most offbeat idea on the page leads to the best solution. Brainstorming is a powerful technique that can help you generate ideas.

THE CREATIVE EXECUTIVE RETREAT

More and more executive management teams seem to be using the *strategy retreat session* as a format for thinking through the direction of the company. This kind of a session, which is preferably held away from the day-to-day work routine, can be extremely productive and valuable if the executives are well trained in CPS methods.

The customary business format has certain disadvantages when we need to expand the thinking processes on a large scale and evaluate a multitude of issues, questions, points of view, options, and relationships. The normal linear structure of a standard business meeting often causes premature closure on issues that deserve a good deal of careful thought. The parliamentary atmosphere that usually accompanies a preconceived topic agenda tends to induce people to take sides on issues too soon.

Too often polarities and positions develop around certain issues, and many important points of view don't get proper consideration. If one person wants to talk about some of the less obvious implications of the topic at hand, the others may be tempted to see that person as digressing or throwing the discussion off the track.

The group may also get lost in a confusing debate on some complex issue with no overall process they can rely on to keep their approach organized. In the extreme, the meeting may become a contest of personalities instead of ideas. A great deal of energy may be expended without producing many concrete outcomes. One person or faction might "win" the meeting in such a situation, but the overall team may not have won.

When questions involving the company's future are at hand, it is crucial to establish an atmosphere of candid problem solving—an atmosphere of open-mindedness, suspended judgment, willingness to explore all productive options, and systematic analysis of alternatives. It becomes important to find a process that will help the executive group explore the core issues of the business creatively and yet systematically. The creative strategy process does this. In its essential form the creative strategy process involves the following features:

1. A secluded meeting environment, with all key people present. The atmosphere should be comfortable and informal.
2. A trained facilitator who can guide the overall process while the executives concentrate on the issues at hand.
3. A large section of wall space, plenty of large sheets of paper, colored markers, and several easel pads.
4. A set of ground rules about open-mindedness, suspended judgment, and freedom to express ideas nondefensively; an unhurried willingness to explore issues in depth.
5. Enough time—two or three days at minimum—to cover a wide range of topics and still reach decisions on major issues, actions, and outcomes.

The creative strategy process involves the use of a *process agenda* rather than a *topic agenda*. Instead of using the standard approach of working through a preconceived list of topics in a traditional business meeting format, the group works its way through a series of processes that uncover the important issues and links them together into a coherent picture of the company's present situation and probable futures.

The group keeps the grand design in mind by working from the big picture downward to the individual operational issues. Thus they have a basis for evaluating proposed programs, alternative approaches, and policy directions in terms of the overall business picture.

The methods used in this creative strategy process involve more structure than brainstorming, but they allow plenty of room for creative thinking and consideration of far-out ideas. One of the basic techniques you can use is the mind map or spidergram discussed in Chapter Twelve. When I conduct a creative strategy retreat for a group of executives from an organization, it works like this:

I put up a huge sheet of paper on the wall and with a felt marker write a simple focus word or phrase in the middle of the paper. This might be something like "Strategy" or "Our Direction." Then I begin by asking *divergent questions* of the group to draw out many different topics, issues, questions, ideas, and options. As the participants throw out ideas, I diagram them with connecting lines, fanning outward in all directions from the starting phrase that interrelates the various ideas and subideas to one another.

This mind map expands rapidly as the executives toss out topics they want to explore during the session. There is no particular attempt to organize the ideas at first; they tend to fall into natural relationships as they are connected into a large, informal network of issues. Anyone who cares to can take a marker and add to the mind map at will. There is no need to have a consensus for a topic to go onto the mind map.

After an hour or two of this explosive generation of information, the executives find themselves looking at the entire landscape of the business. The company's environment—the business issues, the internal issues, and the policy questions—are all there in the form of a giant, collective "brain-dump." But unlike most brain-dumps, this one is organized, at least loosely, into an interconnected set of ideas that are unique to the company's current situation.

At that point the executives pause and begin to consider the various lines of attack on key issues. They want to come out of the meeting with decisions, policy agreements, actions to be taken, and concrete plans. How do they get from this huge, informal picture of the business to a set of outcomes?

The best line of attack will, of course, depend on whatever is looking back at them from the mind map on the wall. Certain key issues may dominate the entire discussion, and they may need to resolve them first. Two or more issues may be interrelated and may need joint consideration. There may be questions about the company's environment they need to consider before they can resolve the major issues. What do they think is happening in their markets? Where is it leading? How does it affect the company? What maneuvers must they consider to deal with the changing environment?

These questions show why a preconceived topic agenda would have been too rigid. The executives needed to get to the point of a common perception of the situation before attempting to resolve isolated issues.

At this point I may suggest a process for prioritizing the issues. This usually leads to a *major-issues agenda,* which is extracted from the elements of the mind map. The major-issues agenda will go up on a new sheet of paper as a permanent reference throughout the session. The remainder of the session involves using our best thinking processes to resolve these major issues one at a time.

For this, we continue to use the mind-mapping process, building a new mind map for each new issue as we attack it. The problem-solving mind map includes the appropriate cluster of ideas as well as a list of the acceptable options; eventually it also includes the chosen course of action.

The outcome of the entire strategy retreat is a final summary mind map that lists the major issues, the decision or resolution reached for each one, the immediate action to be taken, and the name of the executive who will be responsible for the follow-through. By having everyone become highly aware of the process, we stay on the track and manage our time so as to arrive at closure on the major issues by the end of the scheduled session. Special problems or subordinate issues may be delegated for later resolution by smaller task forces so that they will not divert energy from the major areas.

There are many benefits to this creative strategy process:

1. It creates a broader perspective on the various issues.
2. It reduces the effect of strong personalities and dogmatic viewpoints; everyone has a chance to be heard.
3. It minimizes debates and arguments because the mind-mapping process unfolds too rapidly and in too many directions for the group to get stuck on any one point.
4. It gets better solutions and better decisions as a result of a more thorough exploration of the issues.
5. Participants feel a higher degree of ownership of the decisions and directions that result; there is less tendency for the consensus to disintegrate afterward.
6. The intellectual high that invariably accompanies the creative process tends to revitalize the group and build a stronger sense of cohesion.
7. The team effectiveness of the group tends to increase as a result of a shared ethic for candid problem solving and a shared process which they can apply in many other situations.

NOTES

[1]Irving L. Janis, *Victims of Groupthink* (Boston: Houghton Mifflin, 1973).

[2]Alex Osborn, *Applied Imagination* (New York: Charles Scribner's Sons, 1953).

PART THREE

Managing the Creative Corporation

CHAPTER SIXTEEN

How to Train People to Be Creative

"To raise new questions, new possibilities, to regard old problems from a new angle, requires creative imagination."

ALBERT EINSTEIN

It is widely accepted that people do their jobs better as a result of attending training sessions in creativity. Even a brief training experience can equip them with a new sense of the importance of using their heads on the job. It can provide them with a few basic creative thinking techniques for use in everyday situations.

There are relatively few theoretical-psychological studies that "prove" that creativity training has benefits. But the subjective evaluations of many managers and front-line workers who have attended creativity courses is overwhelmingly positive.

People who have had the benefit of creativity training typically report less stress and more enjoyment in their jobs, increased clarity of thought, more and better ideas, and greater flexibility and adaptability in their personal lives. Simple techniques like deferring judgment, option thinking, brainstorming, and improving language habits appeal to them as useful for solving problems and making decisions.

It is surprising, in view of the widely accepted value of creativity training, that more companies do not use it on a much wider scale. Largely because of fuzzy thinking and misconceptions about creativity, the benefits of this kind of training go largely unappreciated. It is a reasonable conjecture that companies willing to invest substantially in "wall-to-wall" creativity training may reap an abundant harvest of new ideas and new energy.

187

We seem to be coming into an era when top executives are more willing to invest aggressively in mass training programs in order to communicate an important message throughout an organization's culture. For example, Scandinavian Airlines System, which is headed by the dynamic young superstar Jan Carlzon, has used mass training on several occasions.

In 1980, when Carlzon launched an ambitious turnaround program at SAS, one of his strategies was to order a two-day training program for every person in the company. He put all 24,000 employees through an intensive personal enrichment seminar that focused on the need to do their jobs more creatively with the customer's priorities in mind.

British Airways chief executive Colin Marshall did a similar thing on an even grander scale. He trained all 37,000 employees around the world through a two-day experience designed to help them become more service-oriented. He did this just to kick off his ambitious Customer First Program, which virtually revolutionized attitudes in the company about pleasing the customer.

Both these CEOs concluded that a multimillion dollar investment in mass training was a cost-effective way to communicate their message. Both of them believed that taking the message directly to the work force would be more effective than hoping that their philosophy trickle down through the organization's middle management structure.

Carlzon made use of mass training again when he wanted people in the company to understand the financial picture. Calling in the personnel people, he said, "I don't think our employees really understand profit and loss. They don't know enough about the financial state of the company to know where they fit in and how their efforts contribute to company profits." He directed that everyone in the company attend a one-day training program designed to teach all of them how to read the company's balance sheet and operating statement.

As education becomes an increasingly important factor in corporate life today, the time may be ripe for company executives to use training in dramatic, stimulating ways to release the creativity that already exists at the front line. Teaching everyone in the company how to think and work more creatively may turn out to be one of the most cost-effective investments possible in terms of increased productivity and greater adaptability at all levels.

MANY WAYS TO LEARN CREATIVITY

There are, of course, other ways to learn creative thinking besides attending a course. Books, videos, listening tapes, and self-study packages can all provide some degree of useful input. Prepackaged programs for people at the work unit level can deliver a degree of learning at a relatively low cost. But few avenues can match the group training experience in terms of the motivation, excitement level, and chance to put what one is learning directly to use. A skilled seminar leader can serve as a role model, source of inspiration, and guide who can clarify and reinforce the important ideas.

Some organizations combine classroom creativity training with special skill-building projects and other personal enrichment experiences to round out the learning process. For example, the Iowa Public Service Company, a progressive power company in the Midwest, conducted an executive creativity program that spanned nearly a year. It included creativity seminars for all senior executives, together with a reading program, personal development retreats, and team creativity projects.

After presenting the wrap-up seminar for the program, I had the pleasure of watching 24 executives in four teams demonstrate their creative design projects in an atmosphere of friendly competition. Chairman of the Board Frank Griffith had given them the assignment of designing, building, and demonstrating a flotation device capable of getting a person across a lake.

I went down to the lake with the executives in the afternoon and watched as the fruits of their team efforts were put to the test. They had developed solutions ranging from simple water shoes to the most remarkable paddle-wheel contraptions. All of them succeeded, at least to some extent. No matter that one entry got stranded in the middle of the lake when its bicycle chain broke, and two others had to go out to rescue it! In an atmosphere of fun, but with an intensity of effort that is uniquely characteristic of executives, they shared the excitement and sense of accomplishment of team problem solving. Every person in the group felt he or she had learned a great deal from the total experience of the program.

HOW WEIRD DO YOU WANT TO GET?

Specific training approaches in creativity seminars vary widely. There is an enormous range of choices in terms of teaching methods, experiential activity, and opportunities to test and apply the techniques of creativity. Probably the most significant factor in the design of a creativity seminar is the relative proportion of unusual or unfamiliar activity as opposed to conventional or academic teaching-learning activity. I refer to this as the "weirdness" factor. There are high-weirdness training approaches, low-weirdness approaches, and some in between; each has its own particular merits. I personally tend to prefer the low-weirdness end of the scale for most businesspeople, but there are ways to use high-weirdness approaches very successfully.

Low-weirdness approaches tend to employ fairly conventional educational situations similar to the classroom settings familiar to most people. This type of training includes such activities as lectures, brief discussions of specific subjects called *lecturettes*, pencil-and-paper exercises, films, videotapes, discussion groups, and group thinking exercises. Other techniques involve coached problem-solving exercises that use specific creativity methods like forced word associations and similar brainstorming exercises. The advantage of the low-weirdness context is that it is familiar and nonthreatening to people who are not accustomed to unstructured social interaction.

High-weirdness training deals with extremely nonacademic experiences, unfamiliar learning processes, and generally "far-out" activities and exercises. This kind of training sets up a new frame of mind on the part of the recipient. The intention is to put people into such an unfamiliar environment that they will be encouraged to behave—and think—in unconventional ways. The point of view here is to make creativity something very different from any other "subject."

High-weirdness classes tend to be strictly experiential, using such techniques as meditation, nonverbal two-person activities, cooperative drawing, group movements like dancing, body sculpture, mirroring, "new age" music and chanting, and manipulating art materials like clay, paper, or paints. The advantage of the high-weirdness approach is its novelty. It exemplifies creativity in the very process of teaching creativity. However, it is often a bit *too* weird for many businesspeople, who may see it as frivolous, not really applicable to their jobs, and too unbusinesslike.

One of my colleagues, William "Ned" Herrmann, who specializes in the more exotic types of teaching methods, observes, "Their eyes usually glaze over after about the first half-hour. If I don't have them for at least two or three days, they leave in a state of shock." Herrmann, a highly creative artist in his own right, is one of the best-known and most effective of the creativity teachers who use high-impact methods. He divides his five-day course into several stages: Preparation, Incubation, Illumination, and an afterclass evaluation he calls Verification.

Herrmann has developed and tested extensively a questionnaire "instrument" which he believes can measure a person's brain dominance in terms of left-brain and right-brain thinking preferences. (See the discussion of this topic in Chapter Six.) The Herrmann Brain Dominance Instrument asks a series of questions about your habits, preferences, hobbies, feelings, and reactions. A trained counselor or seminar leader then scores the questionnaire and presents you with a profile that portrays your thinking-mode preferences.

Herrmann bases much of his creativity teaching on the concept of brain dominance, as disclosed by his questionnaire. "Dominance seems to be the human condition," he notes. "We are right- or left-handed, right- or left-eyed, right- or left-footed, and right- or left-brained. We tend to rely on the functions of one brain hemisphere more than the others. This brain dominance tends to show up in almost everything we do."

Herrmann's objective in his highly experiential workshop is to help people explore and release their right-brain faculties and integrate them more fully with the familiar left-brain processes of everyday life. To do this, he exposes his students to "new age" mood music, involves them in craft activities, leads them through dancelike movements, and has them draw, paint, and sculpt. He also presents them with group problem-solving tasks, which he has them undertake in teams that he has assembled according to their brain dominance profiles.

For example, some teams of people are all primarily left-brained in their thinking patterns; others are right-brained; and still others are mixed—that is, right-brained people and left-brained people together on the same team. The dramatic differences that emerge in the problem-solving styles of the various types of groups help people in the workshop see the impact of thinking styles on every-day work.

Herrmann's objective is not so much to teach as to induce learning. He believes that people can learn profoundly important things by engaging in unfamiliar experiences, even if they can't necessarily put into words what they have learned.

It may be helpful to contrast the approaches I have used for a number of years in teaching creativity with those of people like Herrmann to give some sense of the range of approaches available for creativity training. Although I seldom have the time to conduct a full seminar any longer, some of my most enjoyable experiences have been with a seminar called "Brain Power." In this seminar I would spend either one or two days with a group, helping them expand their creative abilities and apply new thinking techniques to business problem solving.

Every time I conducted the seminar I learned more about creative thinking, reinforced my sense of the importance of creativity in my own life, and had fun working with the group. One of the universal features of almost all creativity seminars, no matter who presents them, is an element of fun. Although they may have a very distinct business focus and deal with important business or organizational issues, the experience is almost always highly enjoyable.

I typically start such a seminar by showing a movie titled *Brain Power*, which is based on my book of the same title and which is narrated by the actor John Houseman. The movie stresses thinking skills and presents the concept of mental flexibility discussed in Chapter Six. Houseman serves as an engaging and highly credible role model for businesspeople who are about to have a meeting.

After the film I give a brief talk or lecturette about creative thinking skills. I like to start by offering a profile of an effective thinker much like the one presented in Chapter 5. Then I ask people to reflect on their own attitudes and habits of thought. Afterward, I use various experiential activities that help to build specific thinking skills identified in the effectiveness profile. A low-weirdness session like Brain Power involves a great deal of emphasis on mental flexibility as an avenue to many other aspects of creativity and effective problem solving.

I like to familiarize people with the automatic processes of their brains and help them become more aware of the differences between divergent thinking and convergent thinking. Using color slides and transparencies that portray various visual illusions and other perceptual phenomena, I illustrate the pattern structures the human mind employs to process experience and show how these patterns can sometimes block effective problem solving. I place a great deal of emphasis on the differences between divergent and convergent thinking processes and use various exercises that highlight the two. Once the group understands each concept, I introduce other exercises that dramatize the power of the imagination. I also show the group how to use brainstorming methods and other mass idea-production techniques.

In the Brain Power session we explore the concept of thinking styles, using *Mindex: Your Thinking Style Profile*, a questionnaire I developed for businesspeople. Using Mindex, a person answers a series of 100 questions about various aspects of his or her thinking habits and skills. He or she then scores the results and comes up with a profile that portrays his or her thinking style in terms of the four patterns described in Chapter Six—Red Earth, Blue Earth, Red Sky, and Blue Sky.

Using the information from their thinking style profiles, people can then analyze their relationships with their bosses, co-workers, family, spouses, and "significant others." They also learn how to assess the combined thinking style of their work team and to understand better how they work and collaborate with their co-workers in business situations.

In addition, I explain the "whole brain" problem-solving technique called mind-mapping, which is a creative way to attack and solve problems by diagramming the relationships that exist among the key factors involved in the problem. (See Chapter Twelve.)

The objective of the seminar, as I see it, is to take the various concepts and techniques—mental flexibility, divergent and convergent thinking, thinking styles, imagination, brainstorming, logical problems solving, and the like—and combine them into a unified problem-solving method. This enables the people who have attended the workshop to go back to their jobs and begin to apply specific methods in the context of business problems they deal with every day.

Of course, there are many options between high-weirdness and low-weirdness approaches. There is room for the more straightforward presentation of information in even the most exotic learning situation, and even the most conventional situation can benefit from some unconventional, energy-raising methods.

THE IMPORTANCE OF FOLLOW-UP AFTER TRAINING

All a creativity training program can ever do is to stir up the members of an organization and encourage them to do their jobs more creatively. Unless the company's managers encourage, reward, and inspire people to think more creatively, the behavior will go back to the old norm.

People in any organization are a part of their environment. If the environment is good for creativity, then creativity will continue. If the reverse is true—if the setting does not encourage and reward creativity—then creative thinking and problem solving will not continue. It is up to you to provide the necessary stimulus to keep the members of the organization motivated and on the right track.

WHO'S WHO IN CREATIVITY TRAINING

Quite a few people and organizations provide creativity training for corporations, but only a few have so far distinguished themselves by special contributions to the field. The people and organizations mentioned in the following discussion are those who have written significant books, contributed important methods, or provided special expertise in the teaching of creativity in the United States.

There may well be people of whom I am unaware who should be on the list, and the list is by no means an endorsement of any particular organization or resource person. It is intended merely to give some idea of the main contributors to the field of creativity training as well as some impression of the various current approaches. The list is arranged in alphabetical order, which unfortunately gives it a bit of an immodest look.

Karl Albrecht & Associates.   Karl Albrecht is the author of *Brain Power: Learn to Develop Your Thinking Skills; Brain Building;* and the *Mindex* model of thinking styles. The San Diego–based firm conducts creative strategy retreats for executives and conducts creativity seminars for business organizations. It also sells videos, books, instruments, cassette tapes, and training materials through its Shamrock Press division for use in creativity training.

Don Edward Beck.   An engaging Texan who is continually working to extend the boundaries of brain/mind theory, Beck presents seminars on advanced topics in human thinking and focuses on how to interpret new biological research findings in terms of their significance for adult learning. He has worked extensively with Dr. Clare Graves's model of cultural evolution and uses this theory to develop training approaches for special applications.

Center for Creative Leadership.   A research and teaching institution in Greensboro, North Carolina, founded with philanthropic resources by the family that made its fortune with Vicks VapoRub, the foundation concentrates on creativity issues related to managerial effectiveness. It conducts research, sponsors conferences, and publishes a quarterly newsletter titled *Issues and Observations*.

Creative Education Foundation.   A research and teaching institution in Buffalo, New York, it has had a long and venerable history since its founding by Dr. Alex F. Osborn, the distinguished father of the brainstorming method of group idea production. The institution concentrates largely on educational issues because Osborn's mission was to promote the teaching of creativity. Under the direction of Osborn's successor, Dr. Sidney Parnes, it publishes various educational materials and sponsors a twice-yearly Creative Problem Solving Institute.

Edward de Bono.   While he is not an American, de Bono merits special mention because of his many contributions to the popularity of creative thinking. A Britisher born in Malta, de Bono has written many books, the most famous of which is *Lateral Thinking: Creativity Step by Step*. He coined the term *lateral thinking* to denote the sudden, creative leap of the mind that escapes the imprisoning effects of the habitual, linear or vertical mode of thought. When he is not traveling about the world teaching creativity, de Bono lives in England and teaches at Cambridge University.

Marilyn Ferguson.   Author and commentator on the development of brain/mind research, Ferguson has written *The Aquarian Conspiracy*, an exploration of new findings about how people think. She also publishes the *Brain/Mind Bulletin*, a newsletter devoted to new topics in creativity and human consciousness.

Jean Houston.   A "new age" researcher, writer, speaker, and performer who is deeply involved in the "human potential" movement. An energetic, charismatic speaker, she combines metaphysical, physical, and psychological theories in her research on education and human development.

Idea Development Associates.   Founded by a retired Army general, Morris "Mo" Edwards, this firm offers training in basic creativity techniques. As a military officer, Edwards recognized the importance of developing the thinking abilities of military people at all levels. After retiring from active involvement with the Army, he began teaching creativity methods in the corporate sector in his program Doubling Idea Power.

Kepner-Tregoe Corporation.   While not as strongly oriented to creative methods as most of the other schools of thought, the Kepner-Tregoe system of rational problem solving has had a wide exposure in the business world. Originated by Charles Kepner and Benjamin Tregoe, authors of *The Rational Manager*, the "K-T" method of problem solving has been taught to many thousands of businesspeople over more than 20 years. The Princeton, N.J., firm also licenses trainers in corporations to teach its methods.

Dudley Lynch.   Another energetic Texan who specializes in brain/mind studies and the measurement of human thinking processes, Lynch has developed a brain profile instrument, the Brain Map, which portrays a person's biological preference for certain modes of cognition. He lectures and teaches seminars on whole brain thinking and also publishes an aperiodic newsletter on brain/mind theory.

Eugene Raudsepp. A teacher, researcher, and writer at Princeton University, Raudsepp is the author of *Creative Growth Games* and a number of other books that provide puzzles and games to challenge and develop creative skills.

Stanford University. For years Dr. James Adams has taught creative problem solving and creative design thinking to engineering and science students at Stanford University in Palo Alto, California. Adams wrote *Conceptual Blockbusting*, a very readable guide to creative thinking in the design process.

Synectics Corporation. Located near Boston, this think tank has over the years distinguished itself by developing and applying special creativity techniques oriented toward the invention process. The *synectics method*, as it is known, is a group process that involves such techniques as imagination, visualization, and use of metaphor in order to develop solutions to a well-stated problem. George Prince, one of the principals in the firm, is well-known for his writings and teachings on the process of inventing.

Roger von Oech. Author of the best-selling *Whack on the Side of the Head*, von Oech conducts relatively high-weirdness seminars for businesspeople on creative methods. A whack on the side of the head, by his definition, is any experience or idea you encounter that startles you into thinking about a situation in a new way.

Mike Vance. A motivational speaker who addresses salespeople and other business groups on the subject of creativity. He appears in various video programs and listening cassettes that deal with the subject of creativity.

Whole Brain Corporation. This firm was founded by Ned Herrmann, a pioneer in whole brain creativity training and the measurement of brain dominance. Herrmann's learning center in Lake Lure, North Carolina, is in a peaceful rustic setting that is well equipped to support the experience of exploring creative alternatives in problem solving. Herrmann is author of the Herrmann Brain Dominance Instrument and creator of A.C.T.—Applied Creativity Training.

CHAPTER SEVENTEEN

Building a Creative Culture: Creativity at the Front Line

> *"To make a great dream come true, you must first have a great dream."*
>
> HANS SELYE

Frank Griffith, chairman of the board of Iowa Public Service Company, stood before his senior executives and spoke to them earnestly. Prior to introducing me as I was about to conduct a seminar on a special aspect of creativity, he conducted a brief "seminar" of his own.

Griffith held up two items for the group to see. Both were new consumer products, and both were very novel in design. One was a battery-powered gas cigarette lighter. At the touch of a button on the side of the shiny cylindrical case, the gas aperture immediately produced a small jet of flame.

The second item was a compact 35 mm camera. Griffith asked, "Who in this room knows very little about cameras?" He selected one of the executives who raised their hands, asked her to come to the front of the room, handed her the camera and said, "I'd like you to take a picture of the group with this camera." After a quick glance at the controls and the liquid crystal display on top of the camera, she was able to take the picture with no trouble.

Both of these are creative, innovative products," said Griffith. "Neither was made in this country. But they could have been, and they should have. We're going to have to start thinking a lot more creatively in American business if we're going to regain our position. And I want all of us in this company to be thinking more creatively about the times ahead. We're in a tough business, and it's getting tougher all the time. There's only one answer: we've got to get smarter."

Frank Griffith typifies the kind of executive who believes in brain power as a capital asset. Leaders like him are not afraid of having people at all levels think for themselves. They welcome it. They are willing to authorize their managers and employees to think for themselves and to reward them for it.

The first chapter of this book raised the question: "Is creativity likely to be the new corporate weapon?" In my view the question remains unanswered. A fair answer would be, "Yes, in some cases." Much depends on the kinds of leaders who emerge in our corporate society over the next few years.

Most likely, more senior executives will entertain the possibility of developing corporate cultures that invite and reinforce more creative behavior on the part of their workers. We may be passing into an era in which subtler values come into prominence. The traditional "Harvard Business School" approach to management may become next-door neighbor to more esoteric approaches based on planned cultural change. Creativity training may become much more commonplace in some sectors of business. Other sectors may be entirely unaffected.

If you're a manager, and you believe that the motif of creativity offers promise for improving the effectiveness of your organization—however you define effectiveness—you may want to think about a systematic planned approach or campaign for building a creative culture. The last unexploited resource in our society is the human brain. I've argued throughout this book that the potential for creative cultures is there; in fact it is *waiting* to be called upon.

In this day and age, with so many people performing "knowledge work," all a manager really does is manage brains. The expression used to be *hired hands.* Now it must become *hired brains.* We need to become more acutely conscious that the mental resources a person brings to the job and the mental processes we allow and encourage him or her to use on the job are the only real assets we have. Everything else merely supports the functioning of human mental processes. As Thomas Edison once said, "The chief function of your body is to carry your brain around."

The success model we've been working with is the idea of the adaptive, creative corporation. The question facing you as a leader, whether you're the CEO of a huge corporation, a department manager, or the head of a small company, is: How do you go about making your particular organization creative and adaptive? How do you transform it into a learning system? How do you build a creative culture?

There are basically five steps to this process:

1. Define the culture you want.
2. Communicate the need to the organization.
3. Remodel the reward system.
4. Remodel the structures.
5. Preach and teach the new values.

DEFINE THE CULTURE YOU WANT

First, make sure you understand the nature of the organizational culture you now have. If you've never thought much about your organization's culture, maybe it's high time you did. Here are some questions to ask yourself:

Authority
>What kinds of people are in charge?
>Are they toxic or nourishing?
>Who makes the rules and how?
>What are the perks of power and authority?
>How much freedom of action do people have?
>How formalized are the rules for behavior?

Values
>What are the *real* driving values that govern
>   day-to-day life and work in the organization?
>How do these driving values get communicated?
>How do they get reinforced?
>Do any of the prevailing values conflict
>   with the business mission?
>Do any of the prevailing values have toxic
>   effects on the people in the organization?

Norms
>What are the most constructive norms
>   operating in the organization?
>Are there any destructive norms?
>How do the destructive norms get established?

How do the destructive norms get communicated
and reinforced?

What are the penalties for violating
organizational norms?

Rewards and sanctions

Who gets ahead in the organization and how?

How are the rewards meted out?

How are the sanctions imposed?

Who does most of the rewarding and
sanctioning in the organization?

As part of your "cultural health check," look to see what evidence there may be of the kinds of negative symptoms mentioned previously, such as alienation, conflict, mediocrity, or despair. If any or all of these conditions exist, then you must begin to look for the causal factors that give rise to them.

You can't legislate alienation or mediocrity or despair out of existence. You must give people reasons to feel involved, proud, and enthusiastic about what they do. Similarly, you can't outlaw conflict. Scolding people for fighting and factionalism won't do much to make them work together. You must give people reasons to collaborate, cooperate, and compromise.

Having determined what kind of a culture you want the organization to have, you must then state clearly and simply what it will look, feel, sound, smell, and taste like in reality. You will have to have a concept for the culture that you can communicate to the middle managers, the infrastructure, and the rank and file.

It may help to dramatize the objective in some way. For example, Lee Iacocca repeatedly declared his view of Chrysler's future in these terms: "I have one, and only one, ambition for Chrysler: to be the best. What else is there?"

Jan Carlzon of Scandinavian Airlines declared, "The only thing that counts in the new SAS is a satisfied customer." British Airways CEO Colin Marshall said, "We are going to be the best airline in the world, and that means putting the customer first in everything we do."

The examples I've just cited are all basically operationally oriented. They all revolve around commitment to the basic business purpose. It often helps to give people some kind of a rallying concept like those in the examples so that they can focus their efforts outward toward success in the environment. All three of the executives quoted have also declared their determination to make the cultures of their respective organizations healthy enough to make the operational mission come true.

COMMUNICATE THE NEED TO THE ORGANIZATION

It is worthwhile to some extent to start explaining to people in the organization what your objectives are for the culture. What, in concrete terms, do you want to change? Do you want more collaboration among divisions, departments, and functions? Do you want more innovative approaches to the production processes of the business? Do you want a greater sense of pride in company, product, and self? Do you want a stronger, more intensive focus on the customer? If so, then say so.

Don't expect much to happen just because you tell people what you want. You will discover just how much of a challenge it really is to change the collective attitudes and behavior of a large number of people. But what you can do by communicating the need to the people in the organization is get them started thinking in the right direction. Some of them will start to move, some will start to think, and most will blink their eyes and continue to behave as they are now behaving.

As a leader or a manager in your organization, *you* must start to behave in a manner that is congruent with the behavior you expect from your employees. The top managers in any organization must *model* the behavior they desire for the rest of the company.

Make it a rule to emphasize and reinforce the authority style, values, norms, and reward/sanction philosophy that you are trying to implement. When you walk through the halls, at the daily meetings you conduct, when you give assignments, make sure people know what you stand for and what you expect of them. It is very important for other people to see you expressing the values you are trying to establish.

All the attitudes and habits of thought mentioned in Part Two—A Crash Course in Creativity—are the same ones you need to model. If you are not mentally flexible, then you can't make the value of mental flexibility believable to others. If you don't have a reasonable tolerance for ambiguity and opinion flexibility yourself, then you can't expect these things from others.

If you often make idea-killing statements when others approach you with new ideas, then you can expect others to practice idea killing as well. Lead by example. Be semantically flexible in your opinions, learn to use idea preparation statements, and encourage the flow of ideas from others. The phrase "What goes around comes around" applies in spades when you are trying to implement a creative philosophy.

If you are the company president or CEO, then you should expect the same behavior you display from your managers. You can't afford to tolerate hypocrisy on the part of your subordinate leaders—saying one thing and doing another. You will lose credibility as a leader if you are trying to sell a new philosophy of openness, creativity, and adaptability while your managers and front-line supervisors fail to follow your lead.

REMODEL THE REWARD SYSTEM

I believe it was Peter Drucker who commented, "You can tell that organizational stagnation has set in when the penalty for success gets to be as great as the penalty for failure." It is probably no exaggeration to say that the reward system in a typical large organization is likely to be substantially out of whack with respect to the goals management has for its growth and performance. Reward systems usually evolve informally, unconsciously, and haphazardly. It is indeed a challenge for top management to get the payoffs in the culture to line up in such a way as to provide powerful incentives for people to behave in ways that contribute value to the organization as a whole.

To remodel the reward system in your organization, you need to sit down with your key leaders and take a long hard look at your reward systems. To do this, you need to ask yourself, "Who gets ahead around here, how, and for what reasons?" Be honest with your assessment, and be honest about the extent to which the culture of your organization is inviting people to act more intelligently about the way they work and whether it reinforces them for it.

You may need to rethink the processes you use for evaluating performance at all levels. You may want to redefine the criteria for getting ahead. You may want to clarify the kinds of behavior you consider effective on the part of your managers, and make their advancement contingent on that kind of behavior. You may need to re-educate managers about the kinds of behavior you want them to reinforce in front-line people.

You need to have a process by which you can single people out for special recognition of their efforts. You may want to build a system of material rewards or benefits with which you can provide meaningful payoffs for excellent work. You also need to create some means by which people can contribute their ideas for better ways to do things, including ways that may be outside the boundaries of their job definitions.

As a start, consider a suggestion system as a way to encourage people to contribute their creative ideas. Suggestion systems have been around for years, but very few companies really seem to get the benefits they should from them. Typically, some obscure, low-ranking functionary hidden away in the personnel department has the extra duty of processing suggestions. This is not the same as having a functioning suggestion system.

In many cases the suggestion system, if it exists at all, is little more than an administrative relic. Someone cleans out the suggestion box once a month, throws away the cigarette butts, soft-drink cans, and candy wrappers that have accumulated there, and puts the few filled-out suggestion forms on a stack.

When the coordinator can get around to it, he or she goes over each of the forms one by one and comes up with a suitable reason why it can't be adopted. Then the form letter goes back to the employee, along with the keychain with the company logo on it and a reminder to keep trying.

It doesn't take long for most of the employees to realize that nobody really cares what they think, and that their harebrained suggestions are only creating more work for somebody in an administrative department somewhere. In such a case the presence of the suggestion box gives the illusion that there is a suggestion system in place, when really there isn't.

Suggestion systems actually have an excellent track record, if you look at the ones that have been implemented in a meaningful way. The National Association for Suggestion Systems, which has about 1,000 member companies and maintains its headquarters in Minneapolis, reports some very impressive statistics for the year 1985. According to the association's figures, member companies received 1.3 million employee suggestions, or 14 for every

100 eligible employees. The companies adopted over 330,000 of the suggestions, or a rate of about one in four.

NASS estimated a savings to the companies that reported their figures in the range of $1.25 *billion* in one year. The companies paid over $125 million in awards to employees, with the average award being over $4,000. NASS reports that the number of suggestions submitted, number accepted, and average net savings have been rising sharply in recent years.

Another simple way to strengthen the reward system for creativity is to create a discussion forum where people can present new ideas without censure and without having to go all of the way up the chain of command. This can take the form of an Inventor's Council, Innovation Committee, or Creativity Forum. This approach has a small group of reviewers especially selected for their breadth of knowledge and imagination, who give people with ideas a sounding board.

The members of the forum must be highly educated, highly motivated people who have a high tolerance for partly baked ideas. Their sole responsibility is to listen to the ideas brought in by anyone in the company, not just from the managers or the supervisors. The process seems to work best when the group does not have approval authority, but just gives feedback. If the members like the idea, they can make recommendations to management. If they don't, they can make suggestions to the inventor about ways to improve it.

A person might have an idea for a new product and new way of doing something or a way to save costs, but the idea may have implications beyond his or her job or unit. These tend to be the most difficult ideas to sell because unit supervisors and middle managers often don't want to be bothered with the messy organizational processes involved. A special forum enables the inventor to go to bat for his or her idea, at least to some extent, without having it killed in the chain of command.

It is important that the chief executive and the various area executives place strong expectations on managers at all levels in terms of dealing with employees who propose new or creative ideas. Of course, they don't have to accept every idea that comes into their offices, but they should be as receptive as possible to any ideas that may contribute to the betterment of the organization as a whole. By modeling the skills of open-mindedness, mental flexibility, positive orientation, and divergent responding, managers can make a huge difference in the attitudes of the people in their organizations toward having and sharing ideas.

REMODEL THE STRUCTURES

Structures, systems, methods, policies, and procedures can imprison people or they can empower them. In most organizations, especially larger ones, there tends to be a dense underbrush of rules and regulations that create the impression that everything must be done according to some recipe or other. When an organization gets bogged down in "system-itis," creativity suffers tremendously.

It is true that all organizations need methods and procedures that promote efficiency and effective use of resources. But they also need a way of rethinking their methods and keeping them flexible.

Review the formal and informal structures of your entire organization, and see whether you have an effective combination of the loose and tight properties espoused by Tom Peters and Bob Waterman, as mentioned in Chapter Four. These properties must be appropriate to your business mission and your plan. They must also be appropriate to the kind of culture you want to have in the organization.

Look at the work procedures around you, and see which ones are unnecessary or wasteful and which ones prevent people from doing their jobs more effectively. See what you can do to eliminate the excessive amount of busy work and wasted time that goes on in your firm. Better yet, invite the employees themselves to find the opportunities.

Take a hard look at your policies and procedures manual. Most large companies have them and most of them aren't worth the paper they are printed on. P&P manuals tend to be too large, too verbose, too detailed, and too preoccupied with legislating things that are better left to common sense. The impression they create of strict conformity to rules can create confusion, resentment, and rigidity on the part of the employees, and a sense of unnecessary ritualism in the culture at large.

Consider building some informal structures and processes to help people get outside the formal linearity of the chain of command. Ad hoc committees, task forces, and interunit working groups can facilitate the kind of exchange of ideas throughout the organization that is very difficult to get through the formal management structure.

Consider using the quality circle approach as a way to encourage communication and creativity among your people. The quality circle method, long known for its use in manufacturing industries, can be used very effectively as a way to stimulate some new thinking about the way people do their work.

In its simplest form, a quality circle is a group of employees, often from a single work area, who meet on a regular basis to identify problem areas associated with their work, use creative problem-solving methods to come up with solutions, and present their recommendations to management for consideration.

Quality circles work best when the people in them are strongly motivated, well trained in creative problem-solving methods, and assisted by facilitators who have had extensive training in group methods. Many companies have used the quality circle method successfully, and many have misunderstood and applied it. Contact the International Association of Quality Circles in Cincinnati if you want to know more about the approach.

Remember not to restrict the entitlement for creative problem solving to just a select group of employees. The message is for everyone in the whole organization. You need to set up a wall-to-wall innovation program, one that emphasizes the need for creativity throughout the company.

CONTINUE TO PREACH THE GOSPEL—FOREVER

Several years before Peters and Waterman's book *In Search of Excellence* made business headlines, Tom Peters wrote an article in *McKinsey Quarterly*, the public relations organ of McKinsey & Company, the consulting firm for which he worked at the time. In that article Peters discussed an executive trait he considered very important. In his view the executives who had the most significant impact on the organizations under their stewardship were those who were "constructively obsessed."

In other words, the truly effective executive was one who had selected one key issue about which to become obsessed. One objective, one mission, one key result area, one factor of overriding importance became the principal focus of attention. He or she would preach and teach that one idea—repeatedly, emphatically, unrelentingly, and determinedly—until people in the organization gradually began to buy into it.

This executive obsession, in Peters's opinion, was the key to getting most of the heads in the organization, including those of the managers, turned in the same direction. Like water dripping on a rock, the message wouldn't go away. It was ever-present, worked into a hundred little nooks and crannies by the cumulative effect of the executive's constant advocacy. Whether the message was product quality, cost effectiveness, closeness to the customer, or anything else, the chief preached it, taught it, and reinforced it faithfully. It became the operational gospel of the organization.

The key, in Peters's view, was that the executive had to stay with one theme long enough for it to take. In so many cases, executives fall for the "theme of the month," and get distracted by the next cosmic idea before the last one has had a chance to soak in. When organizations bounce from one theme to another, people get confused, disenchanted with each new dramatization, and cynical.

If you want to build a creative culture, it had better be a long-term undertaking, not this month's theme. It takes time, energy, money, imagination, determination, and strong leadership to shift the attitude set of a whole organization full of people. You had better be ready for the commitment when you set your sights on an ambitious re-engineering of the culture.

Executives need to preach the gospel at every opportunity. They need to get behind middle managers and supervisors and make sure they understand how to reinforce the message at their levels. Middle managers and supervisors need to work constructively with the people on their teams in order to release the creative potential that is always there.

You might consider using a creativity training program as a mass communication vehicle. You can use a variety of methods to get the point across; you want and expect your people to become more creative when they do their work. Teleconferences, guest speakers, video programs, executive retreats, creativity training seminars, quality circles—all help reinforce the culture of creativity.

A creative culture is not a permanent thing. It needs constant care and feeding. Even after going through a major creativity training program, it is reasonable to expect that most organizations will tend to drift back toward static, introverted, and routinized ways of operating. There must be a continuing process of stimulating awareness, reinforcing the desired behavior and renewing the organizational commitment to creativity and adaptation.

SUGGESTED READING LIST

Here is a list of some additional books and articles that may help you explore the subject of creativity in greater depth.

ALBRECHT, KARL. *Brain Building.* Englewood Cliffs, N.J.: Prentice-Hall, 1984.

_____. *Brain Power.* Englewood Cliffs, N.J.: Prentice-Hall, 1980.

_____. *Mindex: Your Thinking Style Profile.* San Diego: Shamrock Press, 1983.

_____. *Organization Development.* Englewood Cliffs, N.J.: Prentice-Hall, 1983.

_____. *Personal Power.* San Diego: Shamrock Press, 1986.

_____. "Are You Creative?" *Business Week*, September 30, 1985.

BENNIS, WARREN. "Where Have All the Leaders Gone?" *American Society for Training & Development Journal*, August, 1984, p. 31.

BLAKEMORE, COLIN. *Mechanics of the Mind.* Cambridge: Cambridge University Press, 1977.

BLAKESLEE, THOMAS R. *The Right Brain.* Garden City, N.Y.: Doubleday, 1980.

BUZAN, TONY. *Make the Most of Your Mind.* New York: Simon & Schuster, 1977.

CALDER, NIGEL. *The Mind of Man.* New York: Viking Press, 1970.

DE BONO, EDWARD. *Lateral Thinking.* New York: Harper & Row, 1970.

_____. *Wordpower.* New York: Harper & Row, 1977.

FLESCH, RUDOLF. *The Art of Clear Thinking.* New York: Barnes & Noble, 1951.

GERVITZ, DON. *The New Entrepreneurs.* New York: Penguin, 1984.

HAYAKAWA, S. I. *Language in Thought and Action.* New York: Harcourt Brace Jovanovich, 1939.

HERRMANN, NED. "Whole-Brain Creativity." *American Society for Training & Development Journal*, December 1982.

IACOCCA, LEE, *Iacocca*. New York: Bantam Books, 1984.

JANIS, IRVING L. *Victims of Groupthink*. Boston: Houghton Mifflin, 1973.

JOHNSON, WENDELL. *People in Quandaries*. New York: Harper & Row, 1946.

LEE, IRVING J. *Language Habits in Human Affairs*. New York: Harper & Row, 1941.

LEVITT, THEODORE. *The Marketing Imagination*. New York: Macmillan, 1983.

OSBORN, ALEX. *Applied Imagination*. New York: Charles Scribner's Sons, 1953.

PETERS, THOMAS J., and ROBERT H. WATERMAN. *In Search of Excellence*. New York: Warner Books, 1982.

PINCHOT, GIFFORD. *Intrapreneuring*. New York: Harper & Row, 1985.

SPRAGINS, ELLYN E. "For Foote Cone, the Answer Is Still 'Whole-Brain' Thinking." *Business Week*, March 3, 1986.

TOFFLER, ALVIN. *The Adaptive Corporation*. New York: Bantam Books, 1985.

VON OECH, ROGER. *A Whack on the Side of the Head*. New York: Warner Books, 1983.

WONDER, JACQUELYN, and PRISCILLA DONOVAN. *Whole-Brain Thinking*. New York: William Morrow, 1984.

DATE DUE

JUL 0 8 1991			
CIRC	OCT 27 1993		
SM94			